SMALL QUILTS
MADE EASY

Shelly Burge

Bothell, Washington

DEDICATION

To Clint, thank you for twenty-six incredible years filled with every possible emotion,
and for your stubborn belief it would all work out. You always make me believe.
To Vicki—you amaze me. Thank you for your confidence in the abilities I didn't know I had.

CREDITS

President . . . . Nancy J. Martin
CEO/Publisher . . . . Daniel J. Martin
Associate Publisher . . . . Jane Hamada
Editorial Director . . . . Mary V. Green
Design and Production Manager . . . . Cheryl Stevenson
Cover and Text Designer . . . . Trina Stahl
Technical Editors . . . . Cindy Brick/Melissa A. Lowe
Copy Editor . . . . .Tina Cook
Proofreader . . . . Leslie Phillips
Illustrator . . . . Laurel Strand
Photographer . . . . Brent Kane

Small Quilts Made Easy
© 1998 by Shelly Burge
Martingale & Company
PO Box 118
Bothell, WA 98041-0118 USA

Printed in Hong Kong
03 02 01 00 99 98   6 5 4 3 2 1

No part of this product may be reproduced in any form, unless otherwise stated, in which case reproduction is limited to the use of the purchaser. The written instructions, photographs, designs, projects, and patterns are intended for the personal, noncommercial use of the retail purchaser and are under federal copyright laws; they are not to be reproduced by any electronic, mechanical, or other means, including informational storage or retrieval systems, for commercial use.

The information in this book is presented in good faith, but no warranty is given nor results guaranteed. Since Martingale & Company has no control over choice of materials or procedures, the company assumes no responsibility for the use of this information.

MISSION STATEMENT

We are dedicated to providing quality products
and service by working together to inspire creativity
and to enrich the lives we touch.

Library of Congress Cataloging-in-Publication Data
Burge, Shelly.
Small quilts made easy / Shelly Burge.
p.   cm.
ISBN 1-56477-243-8
1. Patchwork—Patterns.   2. Machine quilting—
Patterns.   3. Machine appliqué—Patterns.
4. Miniature quilts.   I. Title.
TT835.B8328   1998
746.46'041—dc21   98-30031
                                                CIP

ACKNOWLEDGMENTS

I would like to express my sincere gratitude to the many individuals who encouraged and supported my quilting adventure:

The sixty amazingly brave students who took my first Miniature Quilts class at QuiltNebraska back in 1986. Have you finished your class projects yet?

Becky Haynes and Jeanne Stark, who said yes when I called. Thank you for your beautiful hand quilting.

Barbara Brackman, Jenni Dobson, and Ann Reimer. Your workshops continue to inspire me.

Donna Burge, a wonderful mother-in-law and binding stitcher.

The Well Round Quilters: Karalene Smith, Ruth Kupfer, Sheryl Jonas, Becky Haynes, and Diane Deahl. You are my quilting sisters and special angels.

Ursula Reikes, Cindy Brick, Melissa Lowe, and Martingale & Company. You have made my dream a reality.

My grandmothers, who guide my journey.
And chocolate. It has made me what I am today.

CONTENTS

PREFACE

WHAT IS IT about small things that touch our hearts in a special way? Think about your reaction to puppies and kittens, doll houses full of tiny furnishings, or sweet little infant clothes. Miniature quilts draw that same type of involuntary response—Awww!

Maybe the reason I'm drawn to small quilts is that I learned to sew on a miniature sewing machine. When I was four years old, my grandmother and I made doll clothes on a hand-cranked toy machine.

My interest in quilting didn't develop until my husband's grandmother gave us two quilts for our first Christmas together in 1972. That inspired me to check out the three quilting books available at the local library. I started sewing fabric scraps left over from making clothes for my family into some pretty ugly quilts.

I became interested in miniature quilts in 1980. In no time at all, I was completely absorbed. Working in a small scale is a practical way to try new techniques and unfamiliar color combinations. Small quilts don't take a lot of time or require a large investment in fabrics; if they aren't a success, I don't feel I'm out anything. Every quilt I've made has taught me something, even if it was a mistake. Especially if it was a mistake!

Miniature quilts are admired for their artistry and beauty. However, it has been said that they are not very practical. It would certainly take a big pile of them to keep you warm on a cold winter night. I believe there are many ways to use small quilts around your home. Of course, they can be finished into hot pads and place mats, but I also enjoy decorating with little quilts. Try arranging a group on a wall or draping one over a piece of antique furniture, like a high chair or baby buggy. Collections of dolls or teddy bears definitely need a quilt or two—you can even combine small quilts with your dolls or bears to create fun centerpiece displays.

Miniature blocks are a wonderful addition to garments, and large quilts can be enhanced by the addition of small blocks. For example, small blocks could make a striking border or become part of a larger block, perhaps the center of a Mariner's Compass or Variable Star. Just because you like to make small blocks doesn't mean you can't have a large quilt.

Let's be really practical. Just think about all the tiny scraps of fabric left from larger quilting projects that could be pieced into miniature quilts. I keep two scrap baskets on my work table: one for fabric strips and one for other pieces. When the creative mood strikes, I sort through the baskets. Sometimes I just dump them out on the table and see if anything sparks an idea.

Promise you won't tell anyone, but my students and I have even been known to forage through trash baskets at quilt conferences to rescue fabric scraps thrown away during workshops. It would be such a shame to see those beautiful fabrics go to waste.

Anyone who is a fabric fanatic, like I am, occasionally has second thoughts about cutting into their special fabrics. Miniature quilts ease our guilt by letting us use small amounts while saving the majority, just in case that perfect project comes along some day.

My fascination with miniature quilts increases with each one I see. As you browse through this book, I hope you find a quilt or two that tugs at your heart. I believe that once you make a small quilt, you won't be able to resist making another. And another. And another . . .

❧ INTRODUCTION

IN THIS BOOK I explain the variety of techniques I use to achieve accuracy and precision in my small quilts. These are the methods that work for me, as I have refined them over the eighteen years I've been making miniature quilts. They are meant to spark ideas and inspire you to rush to your sewing machine to start a new quilt.

The heart of the book contains complete instructions for fifteen quilt projects. They range from the traditional look of Diamond Four Patch on page 40 to the contemporary style of Wild Geese on page 68. The smallest quilt is 11" x 11"; the largest is 36" x 36". Twelve projects are made with quilt blocks no larger than 4" square.

The machine piecing methods I've included work beautifully for small quilts, but you can use them with patterns of any size. If you haven't used freezer-paper templates, cut bias squares from strip units, or made original paper-foundation patterns, the projects in this book will be a great way to experiment. And you can refer back to this book as you use the techniques to create larger quilts.

I hope you enjoy trying these methods, perhaps combining them with your own style of patchwork. Don't worry. I won't be sending out roving bands of Quilt Police to make sure you are doing it exactly as I describe. Try something new and by all means have fun! That's what quiltmaking is all about.

❧ WHAT IS A MINIATURE QUILT?

MINIATURE QUILTS DON'T have to be exact scaled-down versions of full-size quilts. However, they should be well balanced. Everything should be in proportion, including the blocks, borders, fabric prints, and even the quilting thread and batting.

Rules have been established by national quilt contests for what will be considered a true miniature. Most contests set a maximum of 24" x 24" for quilt size. When I first began entering contests, that was basically the only rule. In the last few years, more guidelines have been established. Many organizations now require that miniature quilts be made in proportion or with overall patterns that reflect their reduced scale. Some contests limit the size of the blocks to a maximum of 4" x 4". These rules eliminate quilt designs that feature a 12" x 12" block surrounded by several borders.

Study entry forms carefully before sending your quilt to a national show. Many require that *all* entries have a 4" sleeve stitched on the back for hanging; quilts without a sleeve will not be displayed. While it may seem strange to put a 4" sleeve on a 10" x 10" quilt, it is best to stick to the rules. Unless, that is, miniature quilts are specifically mentioned as an exception to this requirement.

In case you are thinking of making a quilt to fit a tiny bed, a scale of 12" to 1" is the usual proportion for doll-house furnishings. At that scale, a full-size quilt made with 12" x 12" blocks would be reproduced in miniature with 1" x 1" blocks. That's a lot of work for a Bear's Paw block containing forty-five pieces!

FABRICS

Selection

WHEN SELECTING FABRICS for small quilts, I keep one rule in mind. "Would a person looking at a magazine photo immediately realize this piece was a miniature quilt? Or would they have to read the caption to be sure of the size?"

Select prints in proportion to the pieces in the quilt. A design that seems small in a regular-size block can look gigantic when cut into a ¾" square.

Make a "fabric viewer" to see how a print will look when cut into small pieces. With a sharp craft knife, such as an X-Acto, cut a window in a 3" x 5" index card, making the window the same size as the finished piece in the block. Position the card on different fabrics to see what they would look like in the quilt.

Yardage

FOR MY FIRST quilting projects, I bought exactly the amount of fabric called for in the pattern. Gradually I began buying a little extra to add to my collection. Now I love to travel and visit quilt shops. I buy fabrics because the colors or prints appeal to me, usually without any specific project in mind. I decide how much to purchase by thinking about where the fabric might be used in a quilt. For example, if the fabric might make a nice border, I buy two yards. My fabric stash is full of fat quarters (18" x 22") and half-yard pieces; they give me a variety of prints and colors to choose from when I want to make a scrap quilt. When I find an interesting print at a great price, I buy several yards. That way, I have it on hand for backing fabric.

NOTE: *For the projects in this book, all measurements are based on 42"-wide fabric, with a usable cutting area of 40", for insurance.*

Preparation

When new fabrics follow me home, the first stop is the laundry room. I separate the fabrics into darks and lights, then wash them with regular detergent in the machine. I usually toss one of my husband's white handkerchiefs or a white dish towel in with a load of dark fabrics. If the fabric bleeds, I wash it again with a second handkerchief. (My husband has a lovely collection of handkerchiefs in stunning colors.) I put the fabrics through the dryer, then fold them and take them to my sewing room. I wish I could say they are then neatly ironed. Since I really dislike ironing, though, I usually put them away as is. I press them later, just before I start cutting. I sort the fabrics by color and store them in a wire-basket storage system built into a closet. Bifold doors keep out sunlight and dust.

After finishing a large quilt, I often have left-over bias squares and fabric strips. Since I know that particular combination of fabrics works well, I save these scraps separately from the others. I store them in plastic zipper-close bags with a few holes punched in the plastic to allow the fabric to breathe. Later, I can pull out the bag to make a reduced version of the first quilt, or I can use the scraps for a different pattern. Reflections on page 54 was made from scraps left from a queen-size Pineapple quilt. I tend to get carried away when I'm rotary cutting strips.

BASIC INSTRUCTIONS

Accuracy

WHEN MAKING SMALL quilts, accurate cutting and piecing is extremely important. A person making 12" x 12" Nine Patch blocks might never notice if one block is $\frac{1}{16}$" smaller than another. But if a 1" x 1" Nine Patch block is $\frac{1}{16}$" off, it would quickly cause problems. Do you know how many sixteenths of an inch are in 12"? If you answered 192, you win. There are only 16 sixteenths in 1". If a 1" x 1" block is $\frac{1}{16}$" off, it's the equivalent of a $\frac{3}{4}$" discrepancy in a 12" x 12" block. Wow! Strive to be as accurate as possible, and you will be much happier with your finished quilts.

Stitch Length

SET THE STITCH length at ten to twelve stitches per inch when machine piecing small quilts. It is also important to have the correct tension. The line of stitches should run over the fabrics with no loops showing on the top or bottom. If the tension is too tight, the seams will pucker. If it's too loose, the seams might pull apart to reveal the stitches. Either case can affect the accuracy of your piecing.

Seam Allowance

THE MOST FREQUENTLY asked question about small quilts is: "What size seam allowance do you use?" I always sew with a $\frac{1}{4}$"-wide seam allowance, but in some cases, I trim it to $\frac{1}{8}$" *after* stitching. During the many years I've been making small quilts, I've tried piecing with $\frac{1}{8}$" seams. I found they required many adjustments in the templates and rotary-cutting formulas. This was complicated and confusing for my math-deficient brain. It's simpler and more accurate for me to work with the $\frac{1}{4}$" seam allowance that I am familiar with.

Trimming excess fabric from the back of the quilt top creates a better finished quilt. You will find that hand quilting is easier, too. How do you determine if you need to trim the seam allowances? It depends on the size and the number of pieces in the blocks. A 3" x 3" Nine Patch block would not need to be trimmed because there is plenty of space between the seam allowances. On the other hand, a 3" x 3" Log Cabin block, pieced from $\frac{3}{4}$"-wide strips that finish to $\frac{1}{4}$", would require trimming because each $\frac{1}{4}$" seam allowance would meet the next seam line. The entire quilt top would have three layers of fabric, making it difficult to quilt.

The decision to trim seam allowances must be made before you begin piecing. Each seam should be trimmed *after* it is stitched and *before* another seam is sewn across it. Press the seams before trimming (a $\frac{1}{4}$" seam will fold over better then a $\frac{1}{8}$" seam). Trim the seam allowance with scissors, judging the $\frac{1}{8}$" measurement by eye. Or if you prefer, trim with a rotary cutter and ruler.

You can also reduce bulk by removing the fabric "ears" or "tips." These are the little squares that form when one seam is sewn across another. Use scissors to clip across the squares.

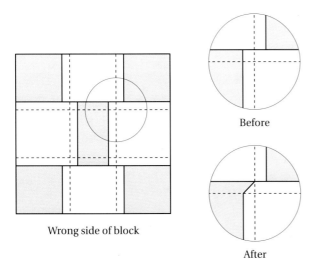

Wrong side of block

Before

After

Pressing

I WANT ANY quilt I make, regardless of size, to lie flat and square. Careful pressing is an important step in achieving that goal. Press each seam toward the darker of the two fabrics before sewing another seam across it. Some quilters press all the seams open in small quilts to distribute the bulk. This also makes sense; small quilts don't get the wear and tear a bed quilt receives, so open seams wouldn't affect their durability. I suggest using the method that works best for you. Occasionally, I do press seams open when sewing one block to another. An example is Reel Friendships on page 48. When sewn block to block, ten layers of fabric meet in one spot!

Templates

I NORMALLY USE rotary-cutting techniques to prepare patches for a small quilt. For odd shapes, such as the leaf pieces in Spring Tulips on page 74, I make templates.

To make accurate templates, draft the block pieces on graph paper. Use a mechanical pencil and drafting ruler to draw the templates, and include a ¼" seam allowance. Cut out the paper template ⅛" *outside* the lines. Using rubber cement, glue the paper template to template material, give it a moment to dry, then cut out the template on the outer (cutting) line. The inner line is your stitching line. You can write piecing information on the paper attached to the template.

If you want to place a template precisely over strip-pieced fabric, draw guidelines on the template to match the seams.

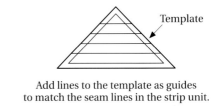

Template

Add lines to the template as guides
to match the seam lines in the strip unit.

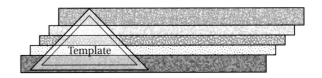

Template

The only template material I use is a laminate distributed by the Flynn Quilt Frame Company. I prefer this material because it's so strong—you won't shave off pieces with your rotary cutter.

That Stubborn Machine

IF I HAD a dime for every time someone looked at the pieces in my small quilts and said they could never do that because their machines would eat up the fabrics, I could have bought a quilt shop by now. They make it sound as though their sewing machines are alive, just lying in wait to gobble up helpless little pieces of calico. Try the following tips to tame your hungry machine.

First, check the needle. How long has it been since it was replaced? If your answer is "during the Nixon administration," it's been way too long. I prefer 80/12 needles for machine piecing. A heavy-duty or dull needle can push the fabric right down into the machine.

Next, check the throat plate. Is it for zigzag or straight stitching? Zigzag plates have a larger oval opening, while straight stitch plates have just a small circle. The smaller opening in the straight stitch plate leaves less room for the fabric to get jammed into. It also seems to provide a more even tension for machine piecing. Look through your machine's accessories, or ask your dealer for a straight-stitch plate.

Chain piecing helps to prevent chewed-up fabrics, as well as thread that twists into a bird's nest when you begin stitching. To chain piece, feed the fabrics through the machine one after the other, keeping a stitch or two between. When you run out of pieces to sew, don't pull the fabrics out of the machine, leaving a tail of thread. Instead, take a fabric scrap (I recommend two layers, each approximately ¾" x 3") and sew across it as the last link in the chain. Leave the "chain spacer" in the machine with the needle down.

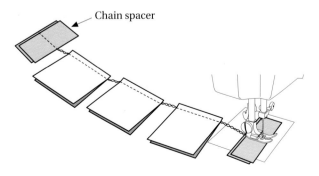

Chain spacer

Clip the thread between the pieces and press. When you return to the machine, the thread will be anchored in the chain spacer. As you begin sewing, the spacer forms the first link in the chain. Each time you come to the end of the chain, sew across the spacer again. This keeps the chain going continuously. You use less thread, and you won't have to refill the bobbin as often.

I use all of these methods, so my machine and I get along great. We even take vacations together.

Tools

THE SIZE OF your quilting tools makes a big difference when you're working with small pieces. You wouldn't use a leaf blower to dry your hair, so why use a 6" x 24" ruler to cut a 1" square? Use tools in proportion to the project. I suggest the following:

Bias Square® ruler: Get a 4" x 4" ruler for trimming blocks. A 6" x 6" ruler is perfect for making strip-pieced bias units and for cutting setting pieces.

Rotary cutters: The cutter with a small wheel is nice for trimming little pieces. Use the large wheel to cut strips.

Rotary-cutting rulers: You'll want a 3" x 22" ruler for cutting strips, and a 2" x 18" ruler, divided in ⅛" increments, for the Stitch and Trim techniques.

Cutting mat: A 6" x 8" mat is great to have beside the sewing machine for Stitch and Trim techniques. You will need a larger mat for cutting strips and borders.

Drafting ruler: Use a lightweight 2" x 18" plastic ruler divided in ⅛" increments. (You won't be using this ruler for rotary cutting—just drafting and design work.)

Mechanical pencil: Keep one handy for drafting templates and tracing patterns. The pencil lines are always the same width, making for the best accuracy.

Laminate: This is the template material I use to make rotary-cutter templates. Refer to "Resources" on page 110.

Rubber cement: Use this to glue graph paper to template material.

Graph paper: I prefer ¼"-grid graph paper. Always check the grid for accuracy by measuring 6" down and 6" across on the graph with a ruler. The grid lines should fall exactly at the 6" mark on the ruler.

Reusable-glue stick: This adheres foundation paper to fabric while you piece, but allows you to pull up and reposition the pieces.

Fabric pens: I prefer Sakura Gelly Roll pens. They make a fine line that won't spread, even when you pause. They're also available in more than twenty colors, a nice plus. *Always* heat-set the ink with an iron.

Freezer paper: Use the plain white type available at the local grocery store.

Quilter's GluTube: This product adheres the seam allowance to the freezer paper for hand-appliqué templates.

Straight pins: When working with small pieces, use small pins with very thin shafts. Heavy-duty pins with large, round heads can disturb the placement of the fabrics. My favorites are extra-fine pleating pins and glass-head silk pins. I keep them in a magnetic pin holder.

Newsprint: I prefer newsprint for foundation piecing; it's easy to sew through and tear off. It comes in wide rolls that can be purchased very reasonably from newspaper offices.

Thread for piecing: I use high-quality, mercerized cotton-covered polyester thread. Unless I'm piecing two dark fabrics together, I sew with light gray or tan thread.

Q-Snap Quilting Frame: I like to use the 11" x 11" frame when working on small quilts.

Flannel board: To make a portable flannel board, buy a 2' x 4' ceiling tile. Using a hand saw, cut it to your desired size—18" x 24" is handy. Sew a flannel slipcover, pillowcase style, to slide over it. Glue or hand sew the open end closed. Your blocks will stick to the flannel. For security, you can pin your blocks in place.

Drafting tape: Place tape on rotary cutting rulers to designate the correct cutting lines. It also holds freezer paper or newsprint steady while tracing patterns. Place on the sewing machine to establish the ¼" seam allowance.

Iron and ironing board: I like to set up the ironing board across the room, rather then beside the sewing machine. Walking over to the iron is about the only exercise I get.

QUICK-PIECING TECHNIQUES

OVER THE YEARS, many quick piecing techniques have been developed, and new ones are introduced almost daily. You may be familiar with these methods, but perhaps you hadn't thought of scaling them down for miniature quilts. What are your favorite shortcuts? Try them for small quilt construction; I think you'll find that they work beautifully. Keep in mind that accuracy is important when using any technique. Don't sacrifice quality workmanship for a quick finish. With practice, you will achieve both.

Lengthwise-Grain Strips

1. Fold the fabric in half along the crosswise grain. Place it on the cutting mat with the folded edge toward the bottom and the selvage edge to the left.

2. To establish a 90-degree angle to the fold, place a Bias Square ruler even with the folded edge. Position a long rotary-cutting ruler to the left of the Bias Square, covering enough of the fabric so the cut will remove the selvage. Set the Bias Square aside and run the rotary cutter along the right side of the long ruler.

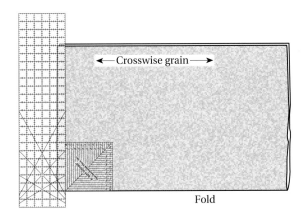

Crosswise grain

Fold

3. Cut strips by matching the measurement line on the ruler with the cut edge of the fabric. After cutting 3 or 4 strips, check the 90-degree angle again by repeating step 2.

4. If both bias- and straight-grain strips are needed, cut bias strips from one end of a fabric piece (see step 2), and straight grain strips from the other.

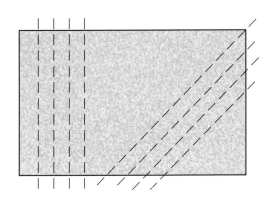

Strip Piecing

The first step in piecing a block is to break it into units. In many cases, there are blocks within a block, as in these traditional designs.

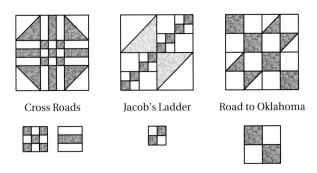

Cross Roads Jacob's Ladder Road to Oklahoma

Simple units can easily be strip pieced. First, cut fabric strips of the required width, including ¼" seam allowances—the strip length is determined by the number of segments needed. Press seam allowances toward the darker fabric, and if necessary, trim to ⅛". For the Four Patch and Nine Patch blocks, cut across the strip units. The cutting width should match the strip width.

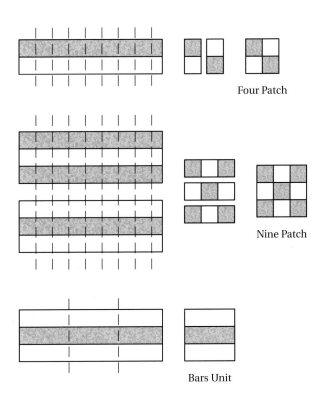

Four Patch

Nine Patch

Bars Unit

Bias Squares

Many block patterns contain bias squares, which may be why there are so many methods for quick-piecing them. One technique is to join two bias strips, then use a Bias Square ruler and a rotary cutter to cut bias squares. The traditional designs shown below all use bias squares.

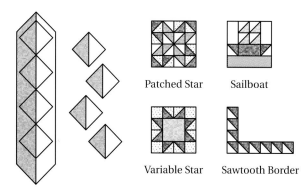

Patched Star   Sailboat

Variable Star   Sawtooth Border

My favorite method for making accurate bias squares is to cut them from bias strip units. To use this technique, cut bias strips the same width as the unfinished bias square. *There is an exception:* For bias squares that are 1½" x 1½" and smaller, you must add an extra ¼" to the strip width. Refer to the chart below to determine bias-strip widths.

Finished Bias Square	Unfinished Bias Square	Width of Bias Strip
½" x ½"	1" x 1"	1¼"*
¾" x ¾"	1¼" x 1¼"	1½"*
1" x 1"	1½" x 1½"	1¾"*
1¼" x 1¼"	1¾" x 1¾"	1¾"
1½" x 1½"	2" x 2"	2"
2" x 2"	2½" x 2½"	2½"

*Extra ¼" added to strip width.

You need a sharp rotary cutter, a large cutting mat, a long ruler (6" x 24" or 3" x 22"), and a Bias Square ruler to cut bias strip units into squares.

1. Layer up to 4 fabrics on a cutting mat, wrong side up, and align the selvage edges. Position the diagonal line of the Bias Square along the selvage and place a long rotary-cutting ruler next to it, as shown.

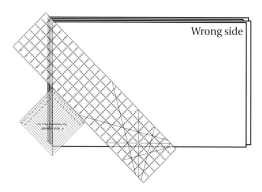

Wrong side

2. Run the rotary cutter along the ruler to make the first bias cut. Measure the width of the strip from the cut edge of the fabric, then cut strips as needed. The length of the strips will depend on the yardage they are cut from. For example, strips cut from ½-yard pieces will be approximately 24" long.

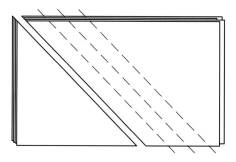

3. To prevent stretching, handle the bias strips with care while sewing and pressing. Sew the strips together with a ¼" seam allowance, alternating dark and light fabrics as you go.

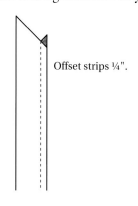

Offset strips ¼".

Short bias strips can be used to fill in the corners, as shown. I press seam allowances toward the dark fabrics when making small quilts, but you can press them open if you prefer. Trim the seam allowances to ⅛" if desired.

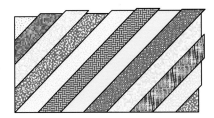

4. Place the diagonal line of the Bias Square ruler along one of the seam lines of the strip unit, and bring the long ruler up tight against the square. Cut off the uneven bottom edge of the strip unit to establish a 45-degree angle.

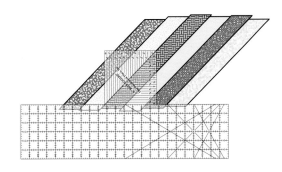

5. Refer to the appropriate quilt pattern for the dimensions of the bias strip segments and bias squares you will cut. Measure the width of the segment from the cut edge of the strip unit. Cut the bias strip unit into segments, as shown. Check the 45-degree angle after cutting every third segment by repeating step 4. If necessary, trim a little off the bottom to correct the angle.

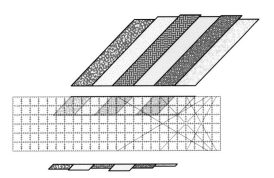

6. One at a time, place the segments on the cutting mat. Position the diagonal line of the Bias Square ruler over the left seam line, with the top edge of the ruler even with the top of the segment. Cut along the right side of the Bias Square ruler. Continue cutting, placing the Bias Square along each of the diagonal seam lines.

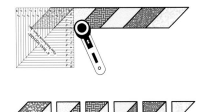

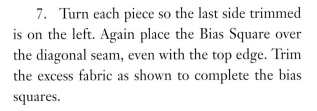

7. Turn each piece so the last side trimmed is on the left. Again place the Bias Square over the diagonal seam, even with the top edge. Trim the excess fabric as shown to complete the bias squares.

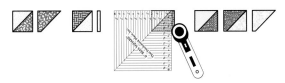

Don't worry if your bias strip units don't look exactly like those shown above. As long as the dark and light fabrics alternate, you can use this cutting method.

Place the long ruler and Bias Square as shown to cut off the uneven edge. Cut the segments as directed. The segments will become longer as you work your way up the unit. Remember to check the angle after every third cut. Cut the segments into bias squares.

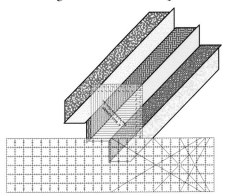

Sew together the scrap triangles and cut a bias square from each. Save the small scraps left between the bias squares for Confetti Appliqué, described on page 85.

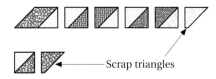

 Scrap triangles

Refer to Zigzag Sampler on page 17 for a variation of this bias-unit cutting method.

Cutting Formulas
Cutting Two Triangles from a Square

To cut two triangles from a square, you must first establish the measurement of the short side of the finished triangle. Add ⅞" to that measurement to determine the size of the square you need. Cut the square in half diagonally to yield two triangles.

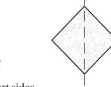

There are two short sides
on a right triangle.

You can also use this formula to cut bias squares into triangles, as shown.

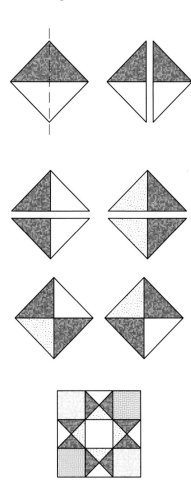

Cutting Four Triangles from a Square

To cut four triangles from a square, you must first establish the measurement of the long side of the finished triangle. Add 1¼" to that measurement to determine the size of the square you need. Cut the square twice diagonally to yield four triangles. The straight of grain in these triangles will run parallel to the long side, unless the square is cut from the bias.

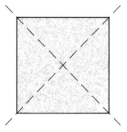 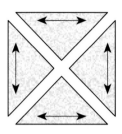

Tip

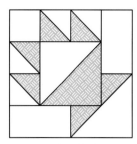

Basket Block

These pieces for the Basket Block can be rotary cut as 4 pieces, then sewn together.

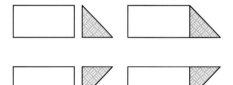

An option would be to strip piece the fabrics and make a template to cut them as one unit. Flip the template to cut a reversed unit. Note the grain lines: one fabric is cut on the straight of grain, the other on the bias.

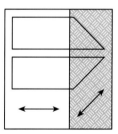

Blocks

WHEN YOU LOOK at quilt blocks, you will find many have elements that can be quick-pieced. If you select one of these blocks when making a small quilt, it will simplify your piecing. Here is a selection of traditional blocks. You can use one or more rotary-cutting techniques to construct each of them.

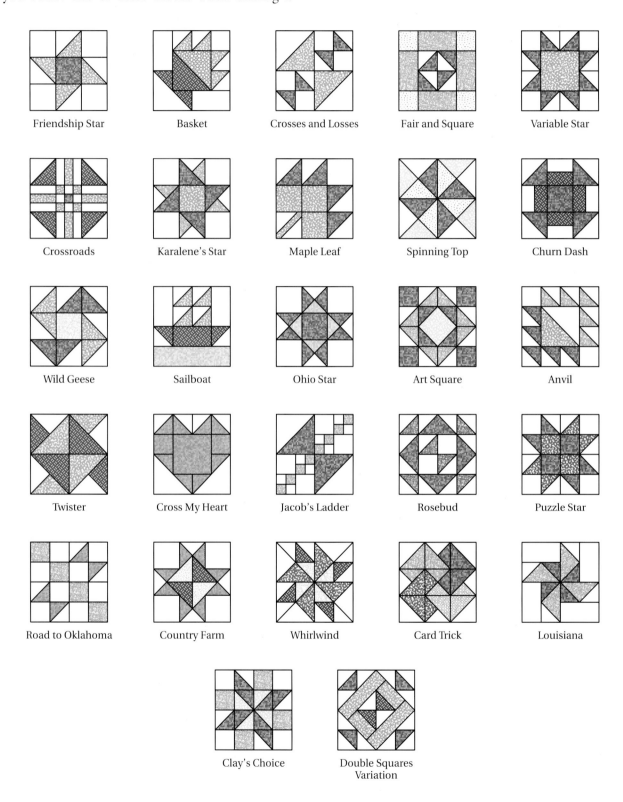

Friendship Star   Basket   Crosses and Losses   Fair and Square   Variable Star

Crossroads   Karalene's Star   Maple Leaf   Spinning Top   Churn Dash

Wild Geese   Sailboat   Ohio Star   Art Square   Anvil

Twister   Cross My Heart   Jacob's Ladder   Rosebud   Puzzle Star

Road to Oklahoma   Country Farm   Whirlwind   Card Trick   Louisiana

Clay's Choice   Double Squares Variation

ZIGZAG SAMPLER

ZIGZAG SAMPLER *by Shelly Burge, 1998, Lincoln, Nebraska, 21¼" x 27⅝". Quilted by Jeanne Stark.*

THE SAMPLER BLOCKS are turned on point in this Zigzag or Streak of Lightning setting. It's not a commonly used pattern, but I think it's very "striking!"

You get to be the designer for this quilt. On page 16, there are twenty-seven traditional quilt blocks to choose from. You need twelve assorted full blocks to make a sampler as shown above, or you can use one block pattern for all twelve

blocks. (Instructions for the twelve full blocks and three half-blocks shown in the finished quilt follow.)

You need one half-block for each of the three vertical sections. These half-blocks are pieced as triangles; they aren't square blocks cut in half. I used scraps left from quick-piecing the full blocks.

DIMENSIONS: 21¼" x 27⅝"

BLOCK SIZE: 3" x 3"

MATERIALS

※

- ½ yd. blue print
- ⅓ yd. black print
- ⅓ yd. red print
- 1 fat quarter (18" x 22") each of 4 tan prints
- ½ yd. green print
- ¾ yd. for the backing
- 24" x 30" piece of batting

Cutting

ALL MEASUREMENTS INCLUDE ¼" seam allowances. Trim the seam allowances to ⅛" after each is sewn to reduce bulk.

Refer to "Block Assembly" for cutting individual pieces.

NOTE: *I've listed all the pieces according to size, in decreasing order. It's important to cut the longest straight-grain strips first. That way, you will have enough fabric to cut the proper length. Use the remaining fabric to measure and cut the bias strips, then shorter straight-grain strips, squares, and so on.*

From the blue print, cut:

- 3 bias strips, each 2½" x 21", for the blocks
- 1 bias strip, 2" x 12", for the blocks

From the black print, cut:

- 2 strips, each 1" x 28", for the side folded accent strips
- 2 strips, each 1" x 22", for the top and bottom folded accent strips
- 2 strips, each 1¼" x 20⅝", for the middle side borders
- 2 strips, each 1¼" x 15¾", for the middle top and bottom borders
- 3 bias strips, each 2½" x 14", for the blocks

From the red print, cut:

- 2 strips, each 1" x 19⅝", for the inner side border
- 2 strips, each 1" x 14¼", for the inner top and bottom border
- 3 bias strips, each 2½" x 16", for the blocks
- 1 bias strip, 2" x 12", for the blocks

From the tan prints, cut:

- 3 bias strips, each 2½" x 21", for the blocks
- 3 bias strips, each 2½" x 16", for the blocks
- 3 bias strips, each 2½" x 14", for the blocks

From the green print, cut:

- 2 strips, each 3¼" x 22⅛", for the side outer borders
- 2 strips, each 3¼" x 21¼", for the top and bottom outer borders
- 3 strips, each 1¼" x 42", for the binding
- 6 squares, each 5½" x 5½"; cut each square twice diagonally to yield 24 triangles for the side setting pieces
- 3 squares, each 3" x 3"; cut each square once diagonally to yield 6 triangles for the corner setting pieces

Preparing Bias Strip Units

AFTER SELECTING THE twelve blocks for my sampler, I realized they required bias squares of five different sizes. I was ready to cut bias strips in five widths when inspiration hit me like a lightning bolt! Instead of making a different bias strip unit for each of the five sizes, I realized that I could cut all the squares from the bias-square unit for the largest size.

If you've chosen different blocks, refer to the chart on page 12 and make a bias strip unit for the largest bias square required, then cut all your squares from that.

The largest bias square needed for the blocks in my quilt was 2⅜" x 2⅜". To simplify cutting the strips, I rounded that figure up to 2½" x 2½".

When you cut small squares from oversized bias strip units, for example, a 1¼" bias square pieced from 2½"-wide strips, there will be a larger-than-usual scrap between the bias squares. Save these scraps to make Confetti Appliqué for "Warm Fuzzy Hearts" (page 84).

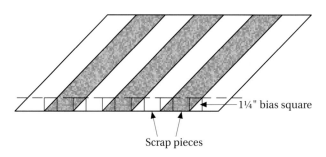

1¼" bias square

Scrap pieces

To make the twelve blocks I chose, make 4 bias strip units as shown. Be sure to mix the four tan prints with the red, blue, and black prints. Cut the units into segments as directed on page 13.

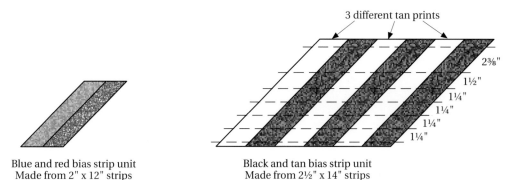

Blue and red bias strip unit
Made from 2" x 12" strips

3 different tan prints

2⅜"
1½"
1¼"
1¼"
1¼"
1¼"

Black and tan bias strip unit
Made from 2½" x 14" strips

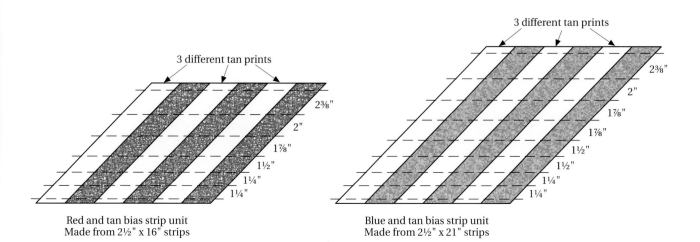

3 different tan prints

2⅜"
2"
1⅞"
1½"
1¼"
1¼"

Red and tan bias strip unit
Made from 2½" x 16" strips

3 different tan prints

2⅜"
2"
1⅞"
1⅞"
1½"
1½"
1¼"
1¼"

Blue and tan bias strip unit
Made from 2½" x 21" strips

Assembling the Blocks

THE INSTRUCTIONS THAT follow are for the full and half-blocks shown in my sampler quilt on page 17. However, you may prefer to replicate one or more of the blocks shown on page 16.

You've already made the bias-square units. Now cut the remaining pieces from your fabric scraps, then sew the blocks together as shown in the illustrations.

For the Anvil block, cut:

- 1 red/tan bias square, 2" x 2"
- 2 tan squares, each 1¼" x 1¼"
- 5 blue/tan bias squares, each 1¼" x 1¼"
- 5 black/tan bias squares, each 1¼" x 1¼"

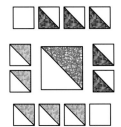
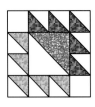

Anvil

For the Basket block, cut:

- 2 tan rectangles, each 1¼" x 2"
- 1 tan square, 1¼" x 1¼"
- 1 tan square, 2⅜" x 2⅜"; cut once diagonally to yield 2 triangles (only 1 triangle needed)
- 1 black square, 1⅝" x 1⅝"; cut once diagonally to yield 2 triangles
- 2 red/tan bias squares, each 1¼" x 1¼"
- 2 blue/tan bias squares, each 1¼" x 1¼"
- 1 black/tan bias square, 2" x 2" (from the 2⅜" strip)

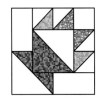

Basket

For the Churn Dash block, cut:

- 1 black square, 1½" x 1½"
- 4 red/tan bias squares, each 1½" x 1½"
- 1 blue and 1 tan strip, each 1" x 6½"

Sew the strips together lengthwise and cut the unit into 4 segments, each 1½" wide.

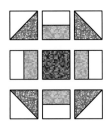
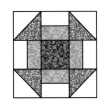

Churn Dash

For the Crosses and Losses block, cut:

- 4 tan squares, each 1¼" x 1¼"
- 2 blue/tan bias squares, each 2" x 2"
- 2 red/tan bias squares, each 1¼" x 1¼"
- 2 black/tan bias squares, each 1¼" x 1¼"

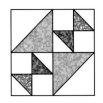

Crosses and Losses

For the Fair and Square block, cut:

- 4 blue rectangles, each 1¼" x 2"
- 4 tan squares, each 1¼" x 1¼"
- 2 red/tan bias squares, each 1¼" x 1¼"
- 2 black/tan bias squares, each 1¼" x 1¼"

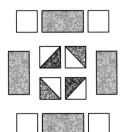
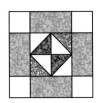

Fair and Square

For the Friendship Star block, cut:

- 4 tan squares, each 1½" x 1½"
- 1 red square, 1½" x 1½"
- 4 blue/tan bias squares, each 1½" x 1½"

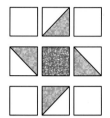 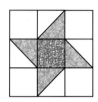

Friendship Star

For the Jacob's Ladder block, cut:

- 4 tan squares, each 1¼" x 1¼"
- 2 blue/tan bias squares, each 2" x 2"
- 1 red, 1 black, and 2 tan strips, each ⅞" x 4". Sew a tan strip to each of the red and black strips. Cut 4 segments, each ⅞", from each strip unit. Sew the segments into 4 Four Patch blocks.

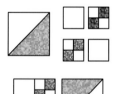 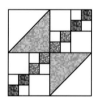

Jacob's Ladder

For the Karalene's Star block, cut:

- 4 tan squares, each 1½" x 1½"
- 1 red square, 1½" x 1½"
- 2 black squares, each 1⅞" x 1⅞"; cut each square once diagonally to yield 4 triangles
- 4 blue/tan bias squares, each 1⅞" x 1⅞"; cut each square once diagonally to yield 8 triangles (4 needed)

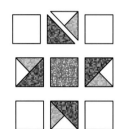 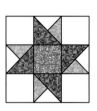

Karalene's Star

For the Ohio Star block, cut:

- 4 tan squares, each 1½" x 1½"
- 1 black square, 1½" x 1½"
- 2 blue/tan bias squares, each 1⅞" x 1⅞"; cut each square once diagonally to yield 4 triangles
- 2 red/blue bias squares, each 1⅞" x 1⅞"; cut each square once diagonally to yield 4 triangles

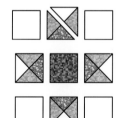 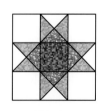

Ohio Star

For the Puzzle Star block, cut:

- 2 red squares, each 1¼" x 1¼"
- 4 tan squares, each 1¼" x 1¼"
- 2 black squares, each 1¼" x 1¼"
- 4 blue/tan bias squares, each 1¼" x 1¼"
- 4 black/tan bias squares, each 1¼" x 1¼"

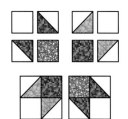 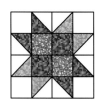

Puzzle Star

For the Spinning Top block, cut:

- 1 red/tan, 1 black/tan, and 2 blue/tan bias squares, each 2⅜" x 2⅜"; cut each square once diagonally to yield a total of 8 triangles

  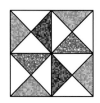

Spinning Top

For the Wild Geese block, cut:

- 1 red square, 1½" x 1½"
- 4 blue/tan bias squares, each 1½" x 1½"
- 4 black/tan bias squares, each 1½" x 1½"

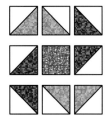

Wild Geese

For the Ohio Star half-block, cut:

- 1 tan square, 1½" x 1½"
- 2 tan squares, each 1⅞" x 1⅞"; cut each square once diagonally to yield 4 triangles (3 needed)
- 1 red/tan bias square, 1⅞" x 1⅞"; cut once diagonally to yield 2 triangles
- 1 blue/red bias square, 1⅞" x 1⅞"; cut once diagonally to yield 2 triangles

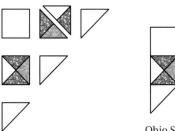 

Ohio Star Half-block

For the Crosses and Losses half-block, cut:

- 2 red squares, each 1¼" x 1¼"
- 2 black/tan bias squares, each 1¼" x 1¼"
- 1 blue/tan bias square, 2⅜" x 2⅜"; cut once diagonally to yield 2 triangles

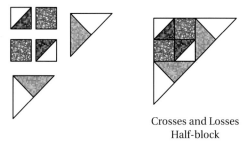

Crosses and Losses
Half-block

For the Pinwheel half-block, cut:

- 1 tan square, 2⅜" x 2⅜"; cut once diagonally to yield 2 triangles
- 2 black/tan bias squares, each 1¼" x 1¼"
- 2 red/tan bias squares, each 1¼" x 1¼"

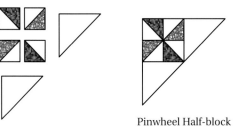

Pinwheel Half-block

Quilt Assembly

1. Arrange the blocks with the setting triangles. Piece the rows in each section diagonally as shown, then join the rows. Sew the 3 sections together.

Section 1   Section 2   Section 3

2. Referring to "Borders" on page 99, sew the red inner side borders to the quilt top. Add the red top and bottom borders.

3. Sew the black middle side borders to the quilt top. Add the black top and bottom borders.

4. Sew the green outer side borders to the quilt top. Add the green top and bottom borders.

5. Referring to "Finishing Techniques" on page 101, prepare a quilt label. Layer the quilt top with batting and backing; baste. Quilt as desired. I quilted my sampler from the back, following the design printed on the backing fabric.

Binding

AFTER QUILTING, ADD the folded accent strips to the quilt top (before binding). This is the same idea as cording, but without the bulk. It adds a dash of color and interest to the quilt.

1. Press each of the remaining 4 black strips in half lengthwise, right sides out.

2. Place the raw edges of the 2 side accent strips even with the sides of the quilt. Machine baste ⅛" from the edge. Add the top and bottom accent strips, and baste in place.

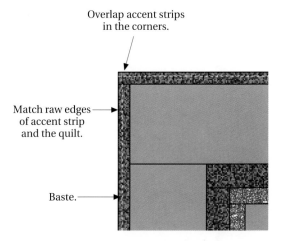

Overlap accent strips in the corners.

Match raw edges of accent strip and the quilt.

Baste.

3. Referring to "Single-Fold Binding" on page 107, bind the edges to finish.

EVENING ON THE FARM

EVENING ON THE FARM *by Shelly Burge, 1997, Lincoln, Nebraska, 18½" x 22½".*

THE BLUE AND brown combination in the Country Farm blocks gives this quilt a soft, "down home" feel. A nice mix of tan prints— including small-scale florals, plaids, geometrics, and stripes—makes up the background.

DIMENSIONS: 18½" x 22½"
BLOCK SIZE: 3" x 3"

MATERIALS

- 6 assorted dark blue prints, each 5" x 5", for the blocks
- 6 assorted dark brown prints, each 5" x 5", for the blocks
- 12 assorted tan background prints, each 7" x 7", for the blocks
- ½ yd. blue print for the borders and binding
- ¾ yd. tan print for the borders*
- ⅝ yd. for the backing
- 20½" x 24¼" piece of batting

Select a fabric printed with stripes, scallops, or rows of flowers.

Cutting

ALL MEASUREMENTS INCLUDE ¼" seam allowances. After sewing, trim each seam allowance to ⅛" to reduce bulk.

From *each* of the assorted blue and brown prints, cut:

- 1 square, 1¹⁵⁄₁₆" x 1¹⁵⁄₁₆", for the blocks
- 2 squares, each 2¼" x 2¼"; cut each square twice diagonally to yield 8 triangles for the blocks

From *each* of the tan prints, cut:

- 1 square, 2¼" x 2¼"; cut twice diagonally to yield 4 triangles for the blocks
- 4 squares, each 1½" x 1½", for the blocks
- 1 rectangle, 1½" x 3½", for the sashing
- 1 rectangle, 1½" x 4½", for the sashing

From the blue print, cut:

- 2 strips, each 3½" x 25", for the side borders
- 2 strips, each 3½" x 21", for the top and bottom borders
- 3 strips, each 1¼" x 30", for the binding

Using the print on the tan border fabric as a guide, cut:

- 2 lengthwise-grain strips, each 2" x 25", for the side borders*
- 2 lengthwise-grain strips, each 2" x 21", for the top and bottom borders*

Cut strips as wide as needed to include the desired designs. Remember to add seam allowances before cutting. The design in my fabric finished to a 1½"-wide border.

Assembly

1. Piece 12 Country Farm blocks as shown: 6 with brown center squares and blue star tips, and 6 with blue center squares and brown star tips. Use tan prints randomly, and try not to use a print more than once in each block.

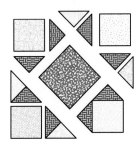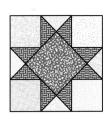

2. Sew one short sashing strip to each block, then one long sashing strip. Arrange the blocks and sashing strips as shown on page 26, step 3.

3. Arrange the blocks in rows of three, turning the blocks as shown, then join the rows.

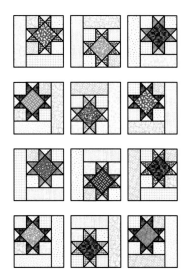

4. Appliqué the tan border strips to the blue border strips. The finished edge of the tan fabric should be ¾" from the inside edge of the blue border strips. Trim the blue fabric under the appliqué to reduce bulk.

Outside edge

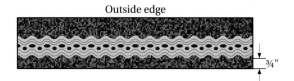

¾"

5. Referring to "Borders" on page 99, sew the borders to the quilt top, mitering the corners.

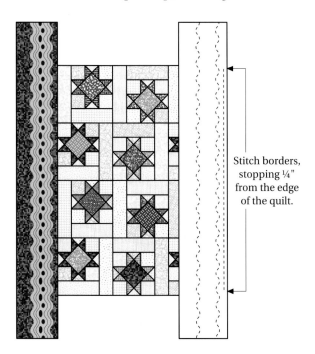

Stitch borders, stopping ¼" from the edge of the quilt.

6. Referring to "Finishing Techniques" on page 101, prepare a quilt label. Layer the quilt top with batting and backing; baste. Quilt as desired, or follow the quilting suggestion. Bind the edges to finish.

Quilting Suggestion

TIP: *If you're using tan thread to machine quilt "in the ditch" between the blocks and blue border, you might accidentally run a few stitches onto the blue fabric. Rather than rip out the stitches, use a permanent blue fabric pen to color the tan thread and make it disappear into the fabric. Press to heat-set the ink.*

Piecing the Borders

❦

You can piece the borders rather than appliqué them; the required yardage is the same.

From the blue fabric, cut:
- 2 strips, each 1½" x 26", for the outer side borders
- 2 strips, each 1½" x 21", for the outer top and bottom borders
- 2 strips, each 1" x 20", for the inner side borders
- 2 strips, each 1" x 14", for the inner top and bottom borders

From the tan print, cut:
- 2 strips, each 2" x 23¼", for the middle side borders
- 2 strips, each 2" x 17½", for the middle top and bottom borders

Fold the strips in half crosswise and mark the centers with a pin. Fold the quilt in half to find the center of each side. Join the strips as shown, matching the centers. Sew the borders to the quilt top and miter the corners.

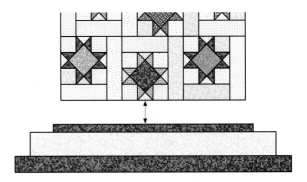

Match centers.

TWINKLING STARS

TWINKLING STARS *by Shelly Burge, 1997, Lincoln, Nebraska, 19" x 20½".*

THE FRIENDSHIP STAR is one of my favorite blocks, so I picked special fabrics to make this quilt. The beautiful hand-dyed Cherrywood cottons were left over from a vest project. (See "Resources" on page 110 for Cherrywood Fabrics' address.) I'm always tempted by the Bali Batik fabrics from Hoffman, and this particular one blended perfectly with the solids.

In some blocks, there isn't much contrast between the solids and the print. This was done deliberately to make the stars "fade" in and out of the background, for a twinkling effect.

DIMENSIONS: 19" x 20½"
BLOCK SIZE: 2¼" x 2¼"

MATERIALS

❧

- 8 fat quarters of 8 different solids
  for the blocks and sashing
- ⅝ yd. directional batik print for
  background, border, and binding
- ⅝ yd. for the backing
- 21" x 22½" piece of batting

Cutting

ALL MEASUREMENTS INCLUDE ¼" seam allowances. Trim the seam allowances to ⅛" after each is sewn to reduce bulk.

NOTE: *Be sure to cut the pieces in the order they are listed; otherwise, you may not have enough fabric.*

From the *lengthwise* grain of the darkest solid, cut:

- 2 strips, each 1¼" x 18", for the inner side borders
- 2 strips, each 1¼" x 16½", for the inner top and bottom borders

From *each* of the 8 solids, cut:

- 1 bias strip, 1½" x 13", for the blocks
- 3 squares, each 1¼" x 1¼", for the blocks
- 3 rectangles, each 1¼" x 2¾", for the sashing strips

From the batik print, cut:

- 2 *lengthwise*-grain strips, each 3" x 18", for the outer side borders
- 2 *crosswise*-grain strips, each 3" x 16½", for the outer top and bottom borders (cut crosswise because of the directional print)
- 4 *lengthwise*-grain strips, each 1¼" x 22", for the binding
- 10 bias strips, each 1½" x 13", for the blocks
- 96 squares, each 1¼" x 1¼", for the blocks

Quilt Assembly

1. Referring to "Bias Squares" on page 12, sew 2 bias strip units, alternating 4 solid strips and 5 batik strips in each. Begin and end with a batik strip.

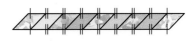

Make 2 bias strip units.

2. Cut 12 bias squares, each 1¼" x 1¼", from each of the 8 solids to yield 96 bias squares.

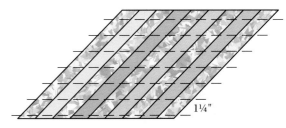

Cut 1¼" bias squares,
8 from each segment.

3. Assemble 24 Friendship Star blocks. I used just 1 color in each block, but you could mix the solids for a different look.

4. Arrange the blocks with the sashing strips as shown. Sew the blocks and sashing strips into rows, then join the rows.

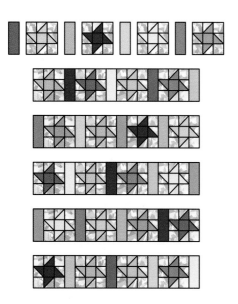

5. Sew 1 inner border strip to each outer border; press the seam allowances toward the outer borders.

6. Sew the top border to the quilt top, stopping 2" from the left edge of the quilt top. Press, then trim the border even with the right side of the quilt.

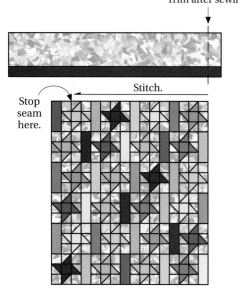

Trim after sewing.

Stitch.

Stop seam here.

7. Sew the right side border to the quilt top. Press, then trim the border even with the bottom of the quilt. Sew the bottom border to the quilt top, press, and trim. Add the left side border, press, and trim. Complete the seam for the top border, then press and trim the border.

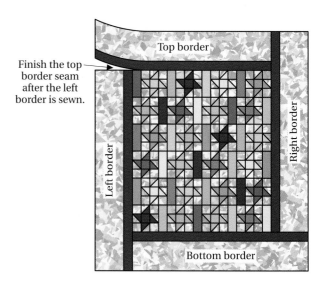

Top border

Finish the top border seam after the left border is sewn.

Left border

Right border

Bottom border

8. Referring to "Finishing Techniques" on page 106, prepare a quilt label. Layer the quilt top with batting and backing; baste. Quilt as desired, or follow the quilting suggestion. Bind the edges to finish.

Quilting Suggestion

CHARMING OLD BLUES

CHARMING OLD BLUES *by Shelly Burge, 1994, Lincoln, Nebraska, 14¼" x 16½".*

MANY YEARS AGO while browsing through a small antique shop, I saw a wonderful twin-size charm quilt. When I asked the clerk about it, she explained the quilt was only on display and not for sale. I was crushed and decided that since I couldn't buy it, I would make it. It took six years to find 123 antique indigo prints, but I finally got my charm quilt. If you don't want to wait six years to start your quilt, make a scrappy variation (see page 34).

I used quick-piecing techniques for the diamond-shaped blocks, rather than time-consuming hexagon and triangle templates. If you are using vintage fabrics to make this quilt, refer to "Antique Fabrics" on page 97 for help before cutting.

DIMENSIONS: 14½" x 16½"

MATERIALS

❦

NOTE: *If you decide to use vintage yardage, make sure to double-check your fabric widths. Vintage fabrics can be as much as half the width of their modern counterparts, so increase the yardage amounts if needed.*

- 87 blue print rectangles, each 1½" x 2", for the Template A blocks*
- 28 blue print rectangles, each 1½" x 2¼", for the Template B & C blocks*
- 4 blue print rectangles, each 1¾" x 2¼", for the Template D blocks*
- 6 blue print rectangles, each 1½" x 1¾", for the Template E blocks*
- ½ yd. cream solid for the block background
- 1 gold solid fat quarter for the inner border
- 1 dark blue print fat quarter for the outer border and binding
- 1 fat quarter for the backing
- 16½" x 18½" piece of batting

*If you prefer, you can quick-cut these pieces from strips. See "Scrap Quilt Variation" on page 34 for instructions.

Cutting

ALL MEASUREMENTS INCLUDE ¼" seam allowances. Trim the seam allowances to ⅛" after each is sewn to reduce bulk.

From the cream solid, cut:
- 12 strips at a 60-degree angle, each 1½" x 20", for the Template A background
- 2 strips at a 60-degree angle, each 1½" x 13", for the Template B background
- 1 strip at a 60-degree angle, 1½" x 8", for the Template D background
- 2 strips at a 60-degree angle, each 1½" x 11", for the Template E background

NOTE: *To cut 60-degree angles, position the 60-degree line of a ruler along the selvage edge of the fabric and make a cut. Measure the width of the strip from the cut edge, and cut again for the strip needed.*

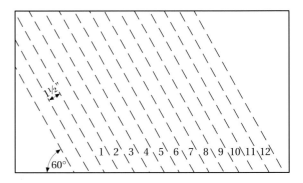

From the *lengthwise* grain of the gold solid, cut:
- 2 strips, each ¾" x 12½", for the inner side borders
- 2 strips, each ¾" x 11", for the inner top and bottom borders

From the *lengthwise* grain of the dark blue print, cut:

- 2 strips, each 2¼" x 13", for the outer side borders
- 2 strips, each 2¼" x 14½", for the outer top and bottom borders
- 4 strips, each 1" x 18", for the binding

Assembly

1. Referring to "Templates" on page 8, prepare the rotary-cutting templates on page 35.

2. Sew twenty-nine 1½" x 2" blue rectangles between four 20"-long cream strips as shown below. Stitching with a cream strip on the bottom to prevent stretching, place the blue rectangles side by side on the strip, one at a time as the strip goes through the machine. Make 3 units. Press the seam allowances toward the dark fabrics.

3. Positioning the guidelines on the template directly over the fabric seam lines, cut 29 Template A diamonds from each strip unit to yield 87 diamonds (85 needed for the quilt).

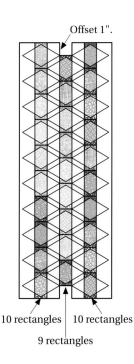

Offset 1".

10 rectangles | 10 rectangles

9 rectangles

4. Make 2 more units by sewing ten 1½" x 2¼" rectangles to one 13"-long cream strip as shown. Cut 10 Template B triangles from each strip unit to yield 20 triangles.

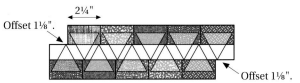

Offset 1⅛".

2¼"

Offset 1⅛".

5. Cut 8 Template C pieces from the remaining 1½" x 2¼" blue rectangles.

6. Sew four 1¾" x 2¼" blue rectangles to the 8"-long cream strip, following the same process as before. Cut 2 Template D and 2 reversed Template D pieces.

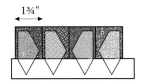

1¾"

7. Sew six 1½" x 1¾" rectangles between two 11"-long cream strips, following the same process as before. Cut 6 Template E pieces.

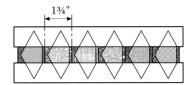

1¾"

8. Arrange the blocks as shown. Sew the blocks into diagonal rows, pressing the seam allowances in alternating directions from row to row. Join the rows.

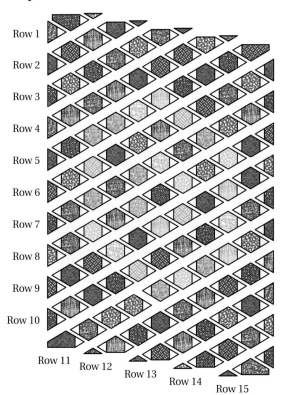

Row 1
Row 2
Row 3
Row 4
Row 5
Row 6
Row 7
Row 8
Row 9
Row 10
Row 11   Row 12
Row 13
Row 14
Row 15

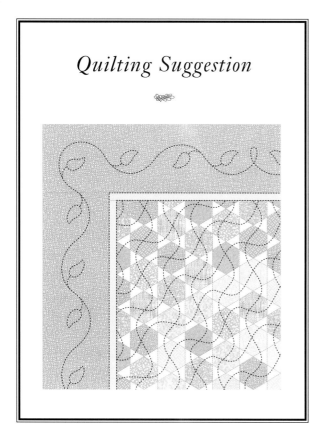

Quilting Suggestion

❦

9. Referring to "Borders" on page 99, sew the inner side borders to the quilt top; press. Add the inner top and bottom borders; press.

10. Sew the outer side borders to the quilt top, then add the outer top and bottom borders, pressing after each addition.

11. Referring to "Finishing Techniques" on page 101, prepare a quilt label. Layer the quilt top with batting and backing; baste. Quilt as desired or follow the quilting suggestion.

12. This quilt has a 1"-wide binding. Machine baste around the quilt less than ⅛" from the raw edge to keep the layers from shifting. Referring to "Single-Fold Binding" on page 107, attach the binding with a generous ⅛" seam allowance. Stop stitching ⅛" from the edges to miter the corners.

Scrap Quilt Variation

INSTEAD OF USING the 125 blue rectangles called for in the Materials list on page 32, cut 9 strips, each 4" x 21", from 9 dark prints. You could buy fat quarters of 9 different dark prints and split them lengthwise with a friend to make two quilts.

From *each* of the 9 dark prints, cut:
- 1 strip, each 1½" x 20", for Template A
- 4 rectangles, each 1½" x 2¼", for Templates B and C (yield of 36; only 28 needed for quilt)

From the assorted dark print leftovers, cut:
- 4 rectangles, each 1¾" x 2¼", for Template D
- 6 rectangles, each 1½" x 1¾", for Template E

Cut the cream, gold, and blue border fabrics as directed on pages 32–33.

1. Referring to "Templates" on page 8, prepare the rotary-cutting templates on page 35.

2. Sew 4 cream strips to 3 dark strips, each 20" long, alternating colors and starting and ending with a cream strip. Sew with the dark strips on top to prevent stretching. Make 3 units, then press the seam allowances toward the dark fabric.

3. Cut 29 Template A diamonds from each unit to yield 87 diamonds (85 required for the quilt), as shown.

4. Follow steps 4–12 on pages 33–34 to finish the quilt.

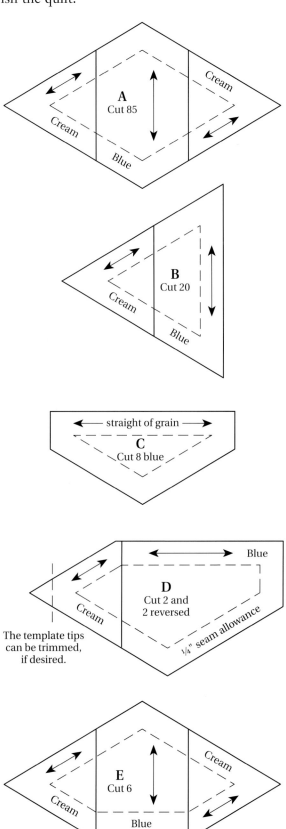

FOLLOW THE
 RED BRICK ROAD

FOLLOW THE RED BRICK ROAD *by Shelly Burge, 1994, Lincoln, Nebraska, 21" x 23¾".*

I USED A QUICK and accurate technique similar to Seminole piecing to create this Stacked Bricks quilt. I selected prints in shades of red, but this pattern would also look great if made with a variety of colors. This is a fast, fun project.

DIMENSIONS: 21" x 23¾"

MATERIALS

❧

- ¼ yd. total of assorted tan prints for background
- ⅓ yd. total of 13 red prints for bricks
- ⅝ yd. black stripe for sashing and inner border*
- ⅓ yd. red print for the outer border
- ¼ yd. black print for the binding
- ¾ yd. for the backing
- 23" x 26" piece of batting

*If you want to use the same fabric for the binding, there is enough yardage to cut lengthwise-grain binding.

NOTE: *The bricks could be pieced from a larger collection of prints. To accommodate additional fabrics, cut the brick fabrics shorter than the 10" called for in the instructions. Sew these shorter brick strips to the tan "cement" fabric and cut into 110 brick segments, as described in the instructions that follow.*

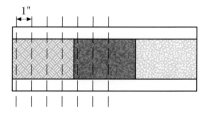

Cutting

ALL MEASUREMENTS INCLUDE ¼" seam allowances.

From the assorted tan prints, cut:
- 26 strips, each 1" x 10", for the blocks (cement)

From each of the 13 red prints, cut:
- 1 strip, each 3" x 10", for the blocks (bricks)

From the *lengthwise* grain of the black stripe, cut:*
- 2 strips, each 1¼" x 18½", for the inner side borders
- 4 strips, each 1¼" x 18", for the sashing
- 2 strips, each 1¼" x 16½", for the inner top and bottom borders

*Adjust the width as needed, according to the repeat of the stripe.

From the *crosswise* grain of the red print, cut:
- 2 strips, each 3½" x 18½", for the outer side borders
- 2 strips, each 3½" x 21", for the outer top and bottom borders

From the *crosswise* grain of the black print, cut:
- 3 strips, each 1¼" x 32", for the binding (or cut 5 lengthwise strips, each 1¼" x 22", from the black stripe, if preferred)

Assembly

1. Sew 2 tan strips to each red strip as shown below. Make 13 strip units. Press the seam allowances toward the tan prints.

2. Cut 9 segments, each 1" wide, from each strip unit for a total of 117 segments (110 needed for the quilt).

3. To make a stacked-brick unit that angles to the right, join 22 segments, offsetting each by ½" as shown. For the row to angle to the right, the bottom brick should feed under the needle *first* as you stitch the units together on your machine. Press all seams in the same direction, being careful not to stretch the rows. Make 3 stacked-brick units that angle to the right.

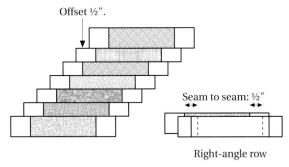

Offset ½".

Seam to seam: ½"

Right-angle row

4. Make 2 stacked-brick units that angle to the left by positioning the top brick to feed under the needle first. Use 22 segments for each unit, and offset each segment by ½".

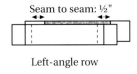

Seam to seam: ½"

Left-angle row

5. Place a ruler across the approximate middle of a stacked-brick unit, from inner point to inner point at a 90-degree angle; rotary cut. (I know it's scary to make this cut, but take a deep breath and go for it.)

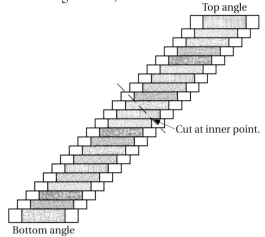

Top angle

Cut at inner point.

Bottom angle

6. Sew the top of the stacked brick unit to the bottom as shown, then press. Cut and join the remaining units.

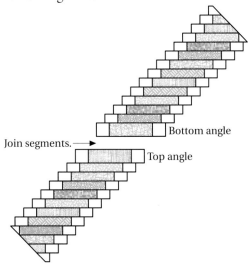

Bottom angle

Join segments.

Top angle

7. Trim the sides of each stacked-brick unit, leaving a ¼" seam allowance. Each unit should measure 2⅝" x 17".

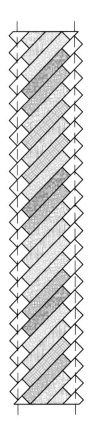

8. Trim each 18"-long black sashing strip to match the length of your brick unit. Fold each sashing strip and brick unit in half, and mark the centers with pins. Arrange the units as shown. Join the units, matching the centers and the top and bottom edges.

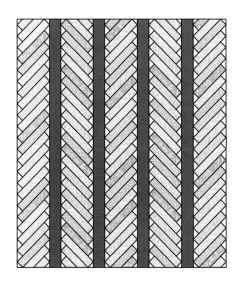

9. Referring to "Borders" on page 99, sew the inner border strips to the quilt top and miter the corners.

10. Sew the outer side borders to the quilt top. Add the outer top and bottom borders.

11. Referring to "Finishing Techniques" on page 101, prepare a quilt label. Layer the quilt top with batting and backing; baste. Quilt as desired or follow the quilting suggestion. Bind the edges to finish.

Quilting Suggestion

DIAMOND FOUR PATCH

DIAMOND FOUR PATCH *by Shelly Burge, 1997, Lincoln, Nebraska, 19" x 21".*

THIS QUILT WAS inspired by an antique doll quilt from the Nebraska State Historical Society's collection. There are forty-one fabrics in my quilt. Most are tone-on-tone monochromatic prints: florals that range from large-scale roses to tiny vines, and stripes, geometric repeats, plaids, and more. I didn't use any solids because they can cause the eye to stop, creating a jarring effect. I cut the diamonds at about 65 degrees because I thought 60-degree diamonds looked too tall and skinny. If you use my method, you don't need a special ruler.

DIMENSIONS: 21" x 23¾"

MATERIALS

✥

- 16 assorted medium tan print strips, each 5" x 12", for the setting diamonds
- ¼ yd. medium brown print for the binding
- 4 assorted light tan print strips, each 1¾" x 10", for the blocks*
- 11 assorted brown print strips, each 1¾" x 10", for the blocks*
- 5 assorted pink print strips, each 1¾" x 14", for the blocks*
- 5 assorted green print strips, each 1¾" x 14", for the blocks*
- ¾ yd. for the backing
- 23" x 26" piece of batting
- Drafting tape

*Cut accurately! These are exact measurements. You may want extra fabric on hand in case of accidents.

Cutting

ALL MEASUREMENTS INCLUDE ¼" seam allowances.

From *each* of the 16 medium tan prints, cut:

- 1 strip, each 3" x 12", for the setting diamonds

From *seven* of the medium tan prints, cut:

- 1 strip, each 1¾" x 10", for the blocks

From the *crosswise* grain of the medium brown print, cut:

- 3 strips, each 1¼" x 40", for the binding

Assembly

1. Draw a 5" x 2¾" rectangle on graph paper as shown. From the bottom right-hand corner of the rectangle, measure 1¼" to the left. Follow that graph line to the top of the rectangle, and mark. Draw a line from the mark back to the corner.

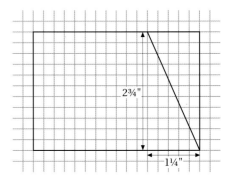

2¾"

1¼"

2. Position the upper edge of a ruler (wrong side up) to the left of the angled line. (A 4½" x 24" or 3" x 22" ruler would work well). Place drafting tape across the ruler parallel with the bottom of the rectangle.

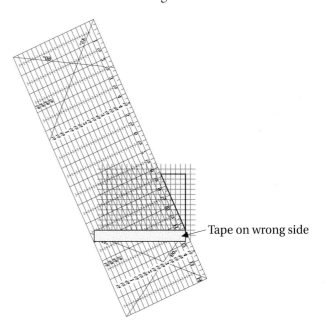

Tape on wrong side

3. To cut the diamond setting blocks, align the ruler's taped line with the bottom of a 3"-wide fabric strip. Trim the right-hand end.

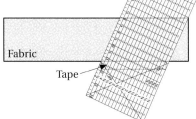

4. Move the angled cut to the left (*right* side up). Measure 3" from the angle and cut. Cut 3 segments from each strip to yield 48 diamond setting blocks.

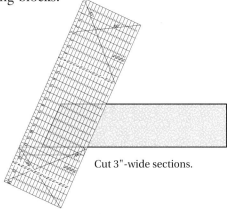

Cut 3"-wide sections.

5. To make the Diamond Four Patch blocks, sew a 1¾"-wide brown strip to each 1¾"-wide medium and light tan strip to make 11 strip units. Press the seam allowances toward the brown print.

6. With the brown strip on the top (right side up), align the ruler's taped line with the bottom edge as shown. Trim the right end of the unit.

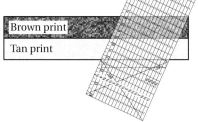

7. Flip the strip unit as shown below, then cut 4 segments, each 1¾" wide, from each unit to yield 44 segments.

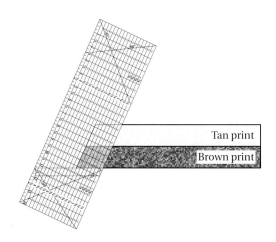

8. Join the segments into 22 brown and tan Diamond Four Patch blocks.

9. Sew the 1¾"-wide pink and green strips together to make 5 strip units. Press the seam allowances toward the green prints. Place the green strip on top (right side up) for the first cut on the right end. Cut 6 segments, each 1¾" wide, from each unit. Sew the 30 segments into 15 Diamond Four Patch blocks (only 13 are needed for the quilt).

10. Arrange the blocks, alternating them with the setting diamonds as shown (refer to page 40 for color placement). Sew the blocks into diagonal rows. Join the rows, then add the corner diamonds.

11. Stabilize the bias edges by machine basting ⅛" beyond the points of the Diamond Four Patch blocks. Trim the edges, leaving a ¼" seam allowance.

12. Referring to "Finishing Techniques" on page 101, prepare a quilt label. Layer the quilt top with batting and backing; baste. Quilt as desired or follow the quilting suggestion. Bind the edges to finish.

Quilting Suggestion

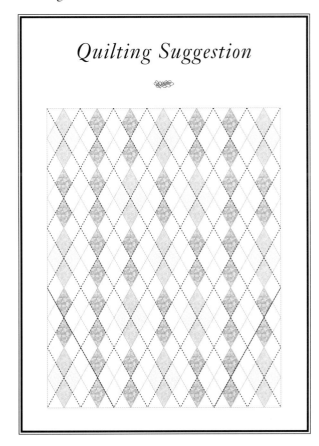

Tip

Occasionally, after I've finished a quilt top, one of the fabrics in it bothers me for some reason. In this case, the Diamond Four Patch quilt had a dark brown leaf print that seemed to catch my eye. At the base of each printed leaf was a distracting white spot. To fix the problem, I got out my handy-dandy fabric pens and colored every white spot. I ironed the quilt top to heat-set the ink. Problem solved—no more white spots.

I've used this solution many times, rather than rip out a fabric. I've even used pens to add designs to fabrics that seemed too plain! I recommend the Sakura Gelly Roll. Always iron to heat-set the ink.

CROW TREES

CROW TREES *by Shelly Burge, 1997, Lincoln, Nebraska, 11" x 11".*

WHEN I SAW the great checkerboard print shown on page 45, I decided to challenge myself to make a quilt using it. It's a Nancy Crow design for John Kaldor Fabrics (now the Balson Hercules Group). The print ranges from pale lemon to rust and has a wonderful shaded texture.

That's right: I made this entire quilt from just one fabric, from the blocks to the binding. I had a ball doing it and finished the top in five hours because I couldn't wait to see how it looked.

Checkerboard and stripe fabrics are perfect for cutting instant bias squares—no need to make strip-pieced units! The Five Patch Tree blocks could be pieced from a variety of prints. If you find an interesting fabric like this one, I hope you will take the challenge too.

DIMENSIONS: 11" x 11"
BLOCK SIZE: 2½" x 2½"

MATERIALS
❧

- 1 yd. checkerboard print (squares should be at least 4¾" x 4¾")*
- 13" x 13" piece of batting

*Your printed squares can be smaller, but make sure they are at least 2" x 2". If you choose the smaller squares, you'll also need a dark and a light fabric, 1 fat quarter of each, that coordinate with the printed squares. Use the fat quarters for the large patches and units.

This fabric used to make Crow Trees.

Cutting

ALL MEASUREMENTS INCLUDE ¼" seam allowances. Trim the seam allowances to ⅛" after each is sewn to reduce bulk.

NOTE: *Keep in mind that the lines dividing the dark and light values run parallel to the straight of grain; a bias square cut from the checkerboard fabric will have four bias edges. Handle the squares with care while sewing and pressing to minimize stretching.*

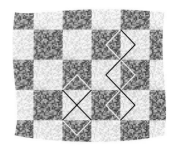

Cut bias squares from checkerboard fabric.

From the checkerboard fabric, cut:
- 56 bias squares, each 1" x 1", for the blocks (piece A)
- 8 light squares, each 1" x 1", for the blocks (piece B)

- 2 dark squares, each 2⅜" x 2⅜"; cut each square once diagonally to yield 4 triangles for the blocks (piece C)
- 2 light squares, each 2⅜" x 2⅜"; cut each square once diagonally to yield 4 triangles for the blocks (piece D)
- 2 dark squares, each 1⅜" x 1⅜"; cut each square once diagonally to yield 4 triangles for the blocks (piece E)
- 4 dark rectangles, each ¾" x 1¼", for the blocks (piece F)
- 4 dark squares, each 1¾" x 1¾", for the center setting square
- 1 dark square, 4¾" x 4¾"; cut twice diagonally to yield 4 triangles for the side setting pieces
- 2 dark squares, each 2⅝" x 2⅝"; cut each square once diagonally to yield 4 triangles for the corner setting pieces
- 4 squares, each 2¼" x 2¼", for the border corners
- 4 strips, each 2¼" x 7½", for the borders
- 2 dark strips, each 1¼" x 24", for the binding
- 1 square, 12" x 12", for the backing

Assembly

1. Fold an F rectangle lengthwise into thirds, then appliqué it to a D triangle. Trim the triangle even with the end of the trunk as shown.

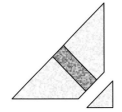

2. Sew an E triangle to the base (short edge) of the appliqué unit. Sew a C triangle to the top (long edge) of the appliqué unit. Make 4 appliqué units.

3. Assemble 4 Five Patch Tree blocks as shown.

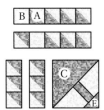

4. Sew 4 dark 1¾" squares together to make the center setting square.

5. Arrange the blocks and setting pieces as shown. Sew the pieces into diagonal rows.

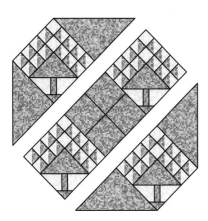

6. Join the rows, adding the corner triangles last.

7. Sew the side borders to the quilt top. Sew the corner squares to the ends of the top and bottom borders, then add the borders to the quilt top.

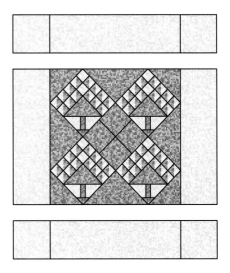

8. Referring to "Finishing Techniques" on page 101, prepare a quilt label. Layer the quilt top with batting and backing; baste. Quilt as desired or follow the quilting suggestion. Bind the edges to finish.

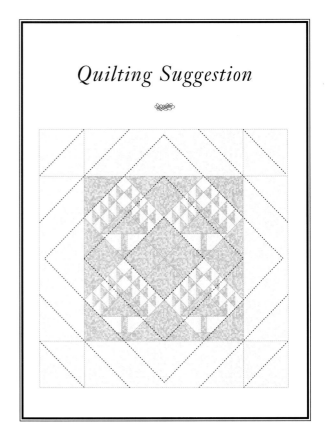

Quilting Suggestion

PRINT VARIATION

IF YOU CAN'T find a checkerboard fabric you like, you could select assorted print fabrics or just one light and one dark print instead.

Materials

❧

- ⅓ yd. total assorted dark prints
- ⅓ yd. total assorted light prints

Cutting

ALL MEASUREMENTS INCLUDE ¼" seam allowances. Trim the seam allowances to ⅛" after each is sewn to reduce bulk.

From the assorted dark prints, cut:
- 3 bias strips, each 1¼" x 17", for the bias squares
- Cut the remaining dark pieces as directed on page 45.

From the assorted light prints, cut:
- 4 bias strips, each 1¼" x 17", for the bias squares
- Cut the remaining light pieces as directed on page 45, including the backing.

Assembly

1. Referring to "Bias Squares" on page 8, make 1 bias strip unit, alternating 3 dark strips and 4 light strips, beginning and ending with a light strip.

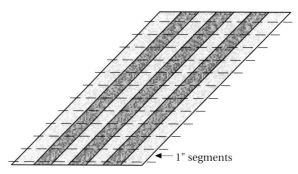

Cut 56 bias squares, 1" x 1".

2. Cut 56 bias squares, each 1" x 1".

3. Refer to "Assembly" on page 46 to finish the quilt.

REEL FRIENDSHIPS *by Shelly Burge, 1998, Lincoln, Nebraska, 20¼" x 20¼". Quilted by Becky Haynes.*

THE VIRGINIA REEL block is a great pattern for scrap quilts. Good contrast between the dark and light values is important, because that's what creates the spinning effect. These blocks are made with a template-free "Stitch and Trim" method.

If you look closely, you may see my "humility" block, with the four patch turned the wrong way. My story is that I planned the quilt that way, and I'm sticking to it.

AUTUMN TRAILS *by Shelly Burge, 1998, Lincoln, Nebraska, 20" x 20". This quilt has a planned fabric arrangement.*

DIMENSIONS: 20½" x 20½"
BLOCK SIZE: 4" x 4"

MATERIALS

- ½ yd. *total* of eight assorted black and dark brown prints for the blocks
- ½ yd. *total* assorted light prints for the blocks
- 1 medium print fat quarter for the border
- 1 black print fat quarter for the binding
- ¾ yd. for the backing
- 23" x 23" piece of batting

Cutting

CUTTING ACCURACY IS very important for the Stitch and Trim technique. Double-check the measurements before cutting, and make sure the centers are square. All measurements include ¼" seam allowances. After sewing, trim each seam allowance to ⅛" to reduce bulk.

From the *lengthwise* grain of the assorted black and brown prints, cut:
- 2"-wide strips, totaling 120", for the blocks
- 1½"-wide strips, totaling 88", for the blocks
- 1¼"-wide strips, totaling 72", for the blocks
- 1"-wide strips, totaling 92", for the blocks

From *each* of the 8 black and brown prints, cut:

- 1 square, 2⅞" x 2⅞"; cut each square once diagonally to yield 16 triangles (1 triangle of each print needed for the border)

From the *lengthwise* grain of the assorted light prints, cut:

- 2"-wide strips, totaling 120", for the blocks
- 1½"-wide strips, totaling 88", for the blocks
- 1¼"-wide strips, totaling 72", for the blocks
- 1"-wide strips, totaling 92", for the blocks

From the *lengthwise* grain of the medium print, cut:

- 8 strips, each 2½" x 13", for the border

From the *lengthwise* grain of the black print, cut:

- 5 strips, each 1¼" x 18", for the binding

Block Assembly

1. From the 1"-wide strips, cut 16 dark and 16 light rectangles, each 2¼" long. Sew 1 dark rectangle to each light rectangle. You should have 16 units, each 1½" x 2¼". Cut 1"-wide segments from the strip units to yield 32 segments. Sew the segments into 16 Four Patch blocks, each 1½" x 1½" unfinished. Each Four Patch should contain 4 different prints.

2. For the first round, use 1"-wide strips. Turn a Four Patch block so that light squares are in the upper right-hand and lower left-hand corners. Sew a light strip to the right side of the block, then sew another light strip to the opposite side. Press all seam allowances in the block away from the center. Use a rotary cutter and ruler to trim the strips even with the Four Patch as shown.

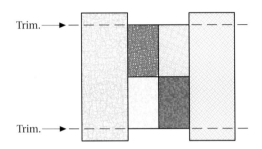

3. Cut two 1¾" long rectangles from the 1"-wide dark strips, and position them on a block as shown. Notice that the dark strips don't extend to the edges of the block. (If you're feeling uncertain about accuracy, you might want to cut the rectangles for the first few blocks slightly longer.) Sew the dark strips to the Four Patch; press.

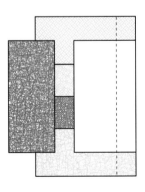

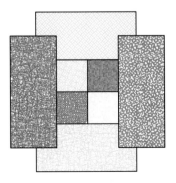

4. Position the 1" line on your ruler so it runs diagonally through the center of the Four Patch. Use the Xs where the stitches cross as a guide. Trim the corner. Turn the block and repeat for the other corners.

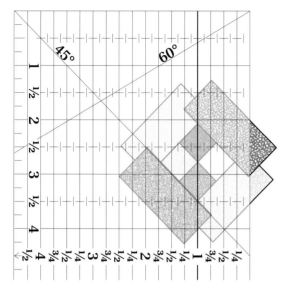

Trim the blocks from the front or back, whichever way you can best see to line up the ruler.

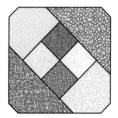

After trimming

NOTE: *After the block is trimmed, the edges will be on the bias. As you continue sewing strips to the block, stitch with the block on the bottom (right side up) and the lengthwise-grain strips on top to prevent stretching. The lengthwise-grain strips will stabilize the bias edges.*

Make sure you don't accidentally square off the points as you stitch. Crisp, sharp points give this pattern its graphic appeal.

5. For the second round, use 1¼"-wide strips. Position the block with 1 light corner triangle in the upper right-hand corner as shown. Sew a light strip to the right side of the block,

then sew another light strip to the opposite side; press. Trim the strips even with the edges of the block.

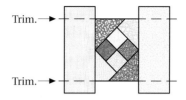

6. Cut two 2¼"-long rectangles from the 1¼"-wide dark strips. Sew them to the 2 remaining sides of the block; press.

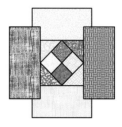

7. Lay the ¾" line on your ruler along the stitching line on the side of the Four Patch as shown. Trim, and repeat for the other 3 corners.

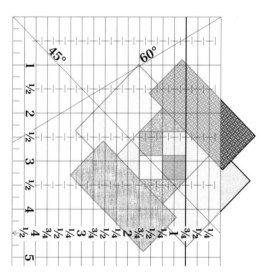

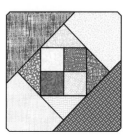

After trimming

8. For the third round, use 1½"-wide strips. Position the block with 1 light corner triangle in the upper right-hand corner. Sew a light strip to the right side, then sew another light strip to the opposite side; press. Trim the strips even with the edge of the block.

9. Cut two 2¾"-long rectangles from the 1½"-wide dark strips. Sew the strips to the 2 remaining sides of the block; press.

10. Place the 1" line on the ruler along the stitches that cross the *point* of the Four Patch. Trim and repeat for the other corners.

11. For the fourth and last round, use 2"-wide strips. Position the block with 1 light corner triangle in the upper right-hand corner. Sew a light strip to the right side and another light strip to the opposite side, then press. Trim the strips even with the edge of the block.

12. Cut 3¾"-long rectangles from the 2"-wide dark strips. Sew the rectangles to the 2 remaining sides of the block, then press.

13. For the final trim, place the 1¾" line on the ruler over the stitches on the side of Four Patch block as shown. Trim and repeat for the other 3 corners.

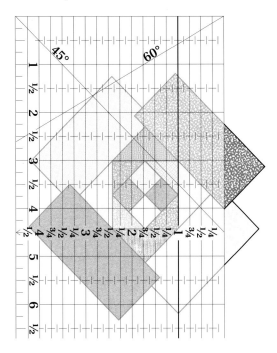

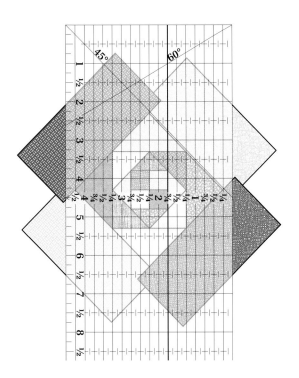

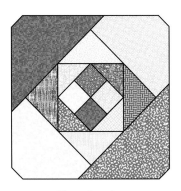

After trimming

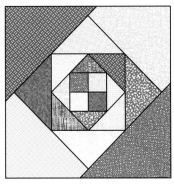

After trimming

14. Repeat steps 2–13 to make a total of 16 blocks.

15. Arrange the blocks as shown. Sew the blocks into rows, then join the rows.

16. For the border, sew together 2 dark triangles as shown. Piece 4 units.

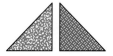 

17. Place two 2½" x 13" medium print strips wrong sides together. Place the 45-degree angle of your ruler along the bottom edge as shown, then trim the strip ends.

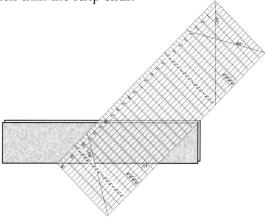

18. Sew the strips to the short sides of the triangle units to make a border unit. Make 4 border units.

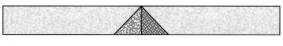

Make 4.

19. Referring to "Borders" on page 00, match the center seams of the quilt top with the center seam of the each border unit, then stitch. Miter the corners.

20. Referring to "Finishing Techniques" on page 101, prepare a quilt label. Layer the quilt top with batting and backing; baste. Quilt as desired, or follow the quilting suggestion. Bind the edges to finish.

Quilting Suggestion

REFLECTIONS

REFLECTIONS *by Shelly Burge, 1991, Lincoln, Nebraska, 23½" x 23½".*

I*N* 1989 I was honored when the Nebraska State Quilt Guild asked me to design their raffle quilt. I created a 103" x 103" Pineapple quilt. Of course I didn't win the raffle (I never win), so I decided to make a miniature reproduction of the quilt for myself. I reduced the 14" x 14" Pineapple blocks to 3" x 3" and scaled down and simplified the original quilting design.

Quilt groups that do annual raffle quilts might consider making a miniature version to keep in their archives. Or perhaps they could award the miniature to the person who sold the most tickets. That would be quite an incentive!

Scrap quilts are my favorites: the more fabrics, the better. That's why there are nearly one hundred different prints in this little quilt.

DIMENSIONS: 22½" x 22½"
BLOCK SIZE: 3" x 3"

MATERIALS

NOTE: *The colors in this quilt connect from block to block to create the overall design. To achieve this, there must be good contrast between the three groups of prints.*

- ½ yd. *total* assorted dark blue prints for the blocks
- ⅓ yd. *total* assorted medium blue prints for the blocks
- 1 yd. *total* assorted light tan prints for the blocks and outer border
- ¼ yd. dark blue print for the inner border and binding
- ¾ yd. for the backing
- 24½" x 24½" piece of batting

Cutting

CUTTING ACCURACY IS *very* important for the Stitch and Trim technique. Double-check the measurements before cutting, and make sure the centers are square. All measurements include ¼" seam allowances. Trim the seam allowances to ⅛" after each is sewn to reduce bulk.

From the assorted dark blue prints for the blocks, cut:

- 28 squares, each 1" x 1", for the block centers
- 34 squares, each 1¼" x 1¼"; cut each square once diagonally to yield 68 triangles for the block corners
- ¾"-wide *lengthwise*-grain strips, totaling 721" in length, for the blocks

From the assorted medium blue prints, cut:

- 1 square, 1" x 1", for the block center
- 12 squares, each 1¼" x 1¼"; cut each square once diagonally to yield 24 triangles for the block corners
- ¾"-wide *lengthwise*-grain strips, totaling 635" in length, for the blocks

From the assorted light tan prints, cut:

- 10 *lengthwise*-grain strips, each 1" x 10", for the outer border
- 20 *lengthwise*-grain strips, each ⅞" x 10", for the outer border
- 26 *lengthwise*-grain strips, each ¾" x 10", for the outer border
- 26 squares, each 1¼" x 1¼"; cut each square once diagonally to yield 52 triangles for the block corners
- 24 squares, each 1" x 1", for the block centers
- ¾"-wide *lengthwise*-grain strips, totaling 1,272" in length, for the blocks

From the dark blue print for the inner border and binding, cut:

- 3 strips, each 1¼" x 35", for the binding
- 2 strips, each ¾" x 19½", for the inner top and bottom borders
- 2 strips, each ¾" x 19", for the inner side borders

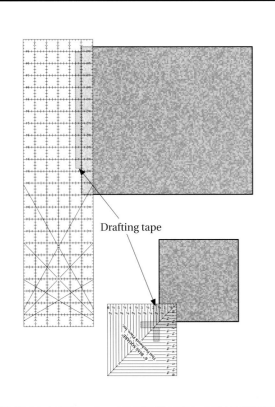

Drafting tape

Tip

❧

*On your rotary-cutting ruler, place a piece
of drafting tape to the side of the measurement line
required. Don't put the tape right on the line;
you still want to see through the ruler to match the line
with the edge of the fabric.*

*The tape will make the cutting go faster.
You won't have to stop each time to find the measurement,
and it helps prevent you from accidentally cutting
the wrong width. The drafting tape can be pulled off and
moved to a new line without leaving any residue
on the ruler. Put drafting tape on Bias Squares, too.
It is available at office and art-supply stores.*

Pineapple Block Assembly

THE QUILT CONTAINS 25 full Pineapple
blocks, 20 Pineapple half-blocks, and 4
Pineapple quarter-blocks, all made with the
Stitch and Trim technique. The color placement
in the blocks is important to the overall design of
the quilt.

When making the blocks, refer to the illustrations at right to help you keep each block type
separate. When the blocks for each type are finished, sort them into piles and label the piles to
avoid confusion.

■ Dark blue
▨ Medium blue
□ Light tan

Block A
Make 1.

Block B
Make 4.

Block C
Make 4.

Block D
Make 4.

Block E
Make 4.

Block F
Make 4.

Block G
Make 4.

Block H
Make 4.

Block I
Make 8.

Block J
Make 8.

Block K
Make 4.

Use the following piecing sequence for Block A, then use it as a guide to assemble Blocks B–H. You might want to make a test block first, using scraps, to teach yourself the process. You'll be much more confident with subsequent blocks.

1. Start with a medium center square and 4 different ¾"-wide dark strips. Sew a dark strip to one side of the center square, then add another strip to the opposite side as shown. Press all seam allowances away from the center square. Using a rotary cutter and ruler, trim the strips even with the square.

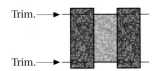

2. Sew a dark strip to each of the 2 remaining sides of the center square; press. Notice that the strips don't extend to the sides of the block. It is sufficient for the strips to extend at least ⅜" beyond the seams. This method reduces the amount of fabric trimmed off the corners, saving you fabric.

At least ⅜"

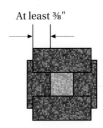

3. To trim the first round, place the ⅝" line on a ruler diagonally through the center square. Use the Xs where the stitches cross as a guide to position the ruler. Take a deep breath, then trim the corner. Turn the block and repeat for the

other 3 corners. Using a Bias Square ruler, make sure the block is square. A crooked block will throw every subsequent round out of kilter.

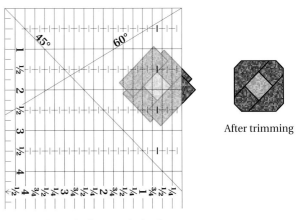

After trimming

Trim from the front or the back, whichever way is easiest to line up the ruler.

NOTE: *The block will have bias edges after it is trimmed. To prevent stretching, sew with the block on the bottom (right side up) and the lengthwise-grain strips on top. The lengthwise grain will stabilize the bias edges.*

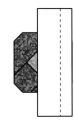

Block is on the bottom.

4. For the second round, use 4 different medium prints. Sew a ¾"-wide strip to one side of the block, then add another strip to the opposite side; press. Trim the strips even with the block.

5. Sew a medium strip to the 2 remaining sides of the block; press.

6. To trim the second round, align the ½" line on the ruler with the side of the center square. Trim the corner. Turn the block and repeat for the other 3 corners. Make sure the block is square.

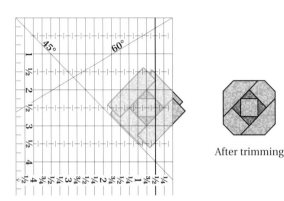

After trimming

7. For the third round, use 4 different dark prints. (You can use the same print more than once in a block, as long as they don't touch.) Sew a ¾"-wide strip to the block, then add another strip to the opposite side; press. Trim the strips even with the block.

8. Sew a dark strip to the 2 remaining sides; press.

9. To trim the third round, align the ½" line on the ruler with the seam that crosses the corner of the square as shown. Trim the corner. Turn and repeat for the other 3 corners. Make sure the block is square.

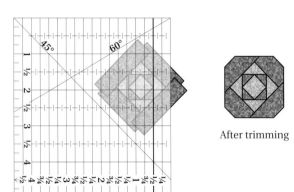

After trimming

10. For the fourth round, use 4 different medium prints. Sew strips to 2 opposite sides of the block; press. Add strips to the 2 remaining sides; press.

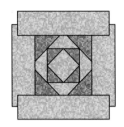

11. The trim measurement for the fourth through tenth rounds is ½". The position of the ruler will change with each round.

For the fifth through tenth rounds, continue adding strips and following the piecing sequence for the earlier rounds. Alternate rounds of dark and medium prints. After 10 rounds, there should be 5 dark and 5 medium alternating rounds, as well as the center square.

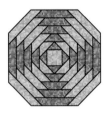

12. For the eleventh round, use 4 different ¾"-wide tan prints. Sew the strips next to the medium strips as shown. To trim, place the ruler in the same position used for the tenth round and use a ½" trim measurement.

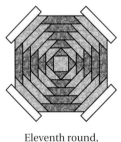

Eleventh round,
before trimming

13. For the twelfth round, sew a different tan print triangle to each corner. Trim as you did for the eleventh round. Check the block to be sure it is square. Block A is finished!

Pineapple Half-Block Assembly

THE PIECING SEQUENCE and measurements for the half-blocks are the same as for the full Pineapple blocks. The difference is that strips are not sewn to all four sides of the center square. Use the following piecing sequence for Block J, then use it as a guide for Blocks I and F.

1. Start with a dark center square and ¾"-wide strips. For the first round, use 2 light strips and 1 medium strip. Sew the light strips to opposite sides of the center square. Trim the strips even with the center.

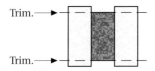

Sew the medium strip to the block as shown. Using a ⅝" trim measurement, cut the 2 corners as directed for the first round of the full block (step 3 on page 57). It's easier to line up the block diagonally if you position it wrong side up.

After trimming

2. For the second round, use 2 dark strips. Sew 1 strip across a corner; press. Trim the strip as shown.

3. Sew the other dark strip to the block. Press and trim.

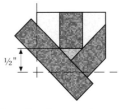

4. For the third round, use 2 light strips and 1 medium strip. Sew the strips to the block as shown. Trim as directed for the third-round trim of the full block (step 9 on page 58).

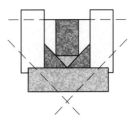

5. For the fourth round, add 2 dark strips. Press and trim.

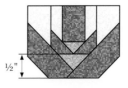

After trimming

6. Continue adding strips until you have completed 10 rounds. Use dark prints to finish the 2 corners with a strip and a triangle, as directed for the eleventh and twelfth rounds of the full block.

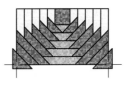

Pineapple Quarter-Block Assembly

THE FOUR QUARTER-BLOCKS (K) are pieced from light prints only. The piecing sequence and measurements are the same as for the full blocks.

1. Sew a ¾"-wide strip to one side of a center square, then trim. Sew another strip to the adjacent side of the center square.

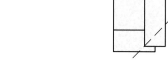

Trim. Trim.

2. For the first round, use a ⅝" measurement to trim the corner. (Refer to step 3 on page 57.)

3. For the second round, sew 1 light strip across the corner as shown. Trim, using a ½" measurement.

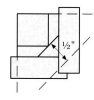

4. For the third round, add 2 light strips and trim as shown.

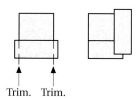

½"

5. Continue adding rounds until there are 10. Finish the corner with 1 strip and 1 triangle. Make sure the block is square.

Trim.

Quilt Top Assembly

1. When the 49 blocks are completed, arrange them as shown below. Refer to the quilt photo to make sure you turn the blocks correctly.

2. Sew the blocks into segments as shown. Join the segments.

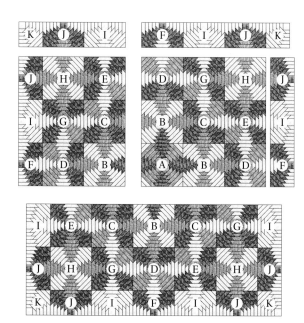

3. Referring to "Borders" on page 99, sew the 2 inner side borders to the quilt top; press. Add the inner top and bottom borders; press.

4. To piece the outer border, sew five 1"-wide, ten ⅞"-wide, and thirteen ¾"-wide tan strips together in random order. Make 2 strip units. Cut four 2¼"-wide segments from each unit to yield 8 segments.

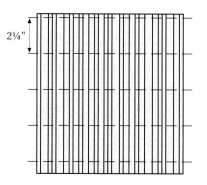

2¼"

5. Sew together segments from each unit to make 4 border sections, each 2¼" x 19½". Flip the segments in opposite directions and mix them up so the border sections are not identical.

6. Use ¾"-wide tan print strips to make 4 corner Log Cabin blocks for the border. Start with a light center square, then add 1 strip. Press and trim the strip even with the square. Add a second strip, press, and trim. Continue in the sequence shown.

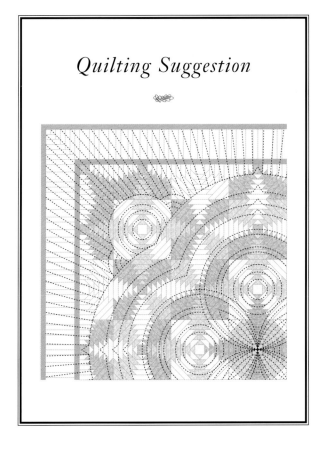

7. Sew a border section to 2 opposite sides of the quilt. Add the corner Log Cabin blocks to the top and bottom border sections. Sew the borders to the quilt top.

8. Referring to "Finishing Techniques" on page 10, prepare a quilt label. Layer the quilt top with batting and backing; baste. Quilt as desired, or follow the quilting suggestion. Bind the edges to finish.

Color Option

PIECE THE PINEAPPLE blocks with just 2 values as shown in the blocks below. Select a mix of tan prints for the lights, and a variety of colors for the darks. Piece 25 full blocks for a 15" x 15" quilt without borders.

Quilting Suggestion

STARRY NIGHT

<small>STARRY NIGHT</small> *by Shelly Burge, 1997, Lincoln, Nebraska, 21¼" x 25¼".*

DON'T LET THE odd shapes, bias edges, and long narrow points intimidate you; this quilt is all straight-line piecing with no set-in angles. Freezer-paper templates work perfectly for a contemporary-looking pattern like this. All the piecing information is written on the templates, which you iron onto the back of each piece, so they're easy to identify. The paper stabilizes the bias edges, preventing stretching. And finally, the edge of the freezer paper is the sewing line, so the pieces don't have to be marked by hand.

DIMENSIONS: 22½" x 25½"

MATERIALS

· 1 yd. shaded blue print for background, outer border, and binding*

· 11 strips, each 7" x 18", from 11 gold prints for stars and inner border

· ¾ yd. for the backing

· 24½" x 27½" piece of batting

*The background fabric in Starry Night fades from dark blue down the middle to pale blue at the selvages. The cut pieces were arranged to shade from dark at the top of the quilt to light at the bottom. If you can't find a commercial print that shades from light to dark, you can probably find a hand-dyed fabric.

STARS OF THE 30S *by Shelly Burge, 1998, Lincoln, Nebraska, 21¼" x 24¼". I made this quilt from the Starry Night pattern. The background fabric is a 1940s feed sack; the stars are pieced from 1930s reproduction prints.*

Cutting

ALL MEASUREMENTS INCLUDE ¼" seam allowances. Trim the seam allowances to ⅛" after each is sewn to reduce bulk. The full-size pattern for Starry Night is on the pullout.

From the shaded blue print, cut:
- 1 *lengthwise*-grain strip of the darkest blue, 3½" x 22½", for the outer top border
- 1 *lengthwise*-grain strip of the lightest blue, 3½" x 22½", for the outer bottom border
- 1 *lengthwise*-grain strip of the darkest blue, 1¼" x 24", for the top binding
- 1 *lengthwise*-grain strip of the lightest blue, 1¼" x 24", for the bottom binding
- 2 *crosswise*-grain strips that shade from dark to light, each 3½" x 19½", for the outer side borders.
- 2 *crosswise*-grain strips that shade from dark to light, each 1¼" x 27", for the side binding.

From *each* of 6 gold prints, cut:
- 1 strip, 1½" x 17", for the pieced inner border

Freezer-Paper Templates

THE FREEZER-PAPER templates are ironed to the wrong side of the fabric. This means that the finished quilt will be the mirror image of the pattern.

1. To make the freezer-paper templates, tape the pullout pattern to a light box or window. Place a large sheet of freezer paper, shiny side down, over the pattern and tape securely. Trace the pattern lines on the freezer paper with a mechanical pencil and drafting ruler. Copy the identification letters, numbers, and grain lines onto each template. Use paper scissors to cut out the templates on the pencil lines.

2. You need to cut 4 star templates from *each* of the 11 gold prints, to yield 44 pieces. Make a cutting guide by pinning a small piece of each gold print to a corresponding star on the pullout pattern. Place the lightest fabric in a star at the top of the quilt, then shade to the darkest fabric at the bottom. Place the 4 templates for each star on the wrong side of a gold fabric, shiny side down. *The templates do not include seam allowances, so be sure to leave room between them for adding ¼" seam allowances as you cut.*

3. On a firm ironing surface, use a dry iron on the highest setting to adhere the templates to the fabric. Cut out each piece, adding an approximate ¼" seam allowance as you go. (The seam allowance doesn't have to be exact.)

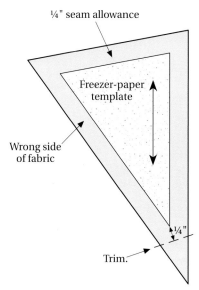

4. Lay the shaded blue fabric wrong side up. Place the templates for the background pieces on the fabric, shiny side down. Arrange the templates so the background will shade from

dark at the top to light at the bottom. Leave room for seam allowances.

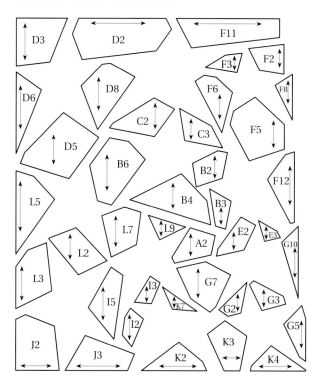

5. Press the templates with a dry iron, then cut out each background piece, estimating the ¼" seam allowance as you go. Leave a generous ¼" seam allowance on the side of each template that will be on an outer edge of the quilt.

Block Assembly

1. Group the templates with matching letters together; they will be pieced as units. I use the "pin and poke" method when lining up 2 pieces. Place a pin in the corners of the templates to line up the top and bottom pieces as shown. Run a pin next to the paper to be sure the template underneath is in the correct position.

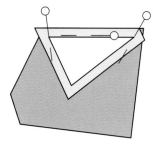

2. Use the following sequence to piece unit D, then use it as a guide to assemble the other units. The freezer paper marks the sewing line, so stitch right alongside it. If a template comes loose, press it again.

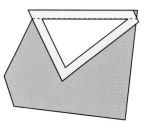

Sew next to the paper.
It is not necessary to backstitch.

Sew D1 to D2; press the seam allowance toward 2. Add D3 to D1; press toward 3. Sew D4 to D5; press toward 5. Sew D6 to D4; press toward 6. Sew D7 to D8; press toward 8. Sew D9 to D8; press toward 8. Stitch the D7-8-9 section to D10; press toward 10. Sew D4-5-6 in place; press toward 4. Add the D1-2-3 section last, and press toward 1. That completes unit D. Don't remove the paper yet!

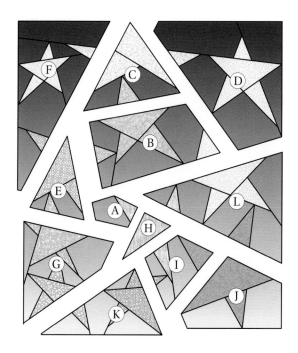

3. After all the units have been pieced, the next step is to have a soft drink and a couple chocolate chip cookies. Walk around and stretch a little before sewing the rest of the block together.

Sew unit A to unit B with a partial seam, as marked by the dot on the pattern. Sew unit C to unit B. Add Unit D to the A-B-C section. Sew unit E to the A-B-C-D section, then add unit F. Add unit G and then Template H. Set the large section aside and sew unit I to unit J. Add unit K to the I-J section. Sew the I-J-K section to the large section. Sew unit L to the large section. Go back and finish sewing the seam between A and B, which now extends along L.

4. To leave a ¼" seam allowance, place the ¼" line of a ruler along the edge of the freezer paper and trim each side of the block. Carefully remove the paper templates; they can be used again. I've used freezer paper templates as often as 7 times.

5. Sew the 6 gold strips together, alternating darks and lights. Cut the strip unit into 11 segments, each 1½" wide.

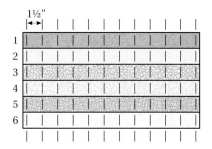

6. Arrange the segments clockwise around the quilt top, repeating the colors in the order shown. Rip out seams as needed to turn corners.

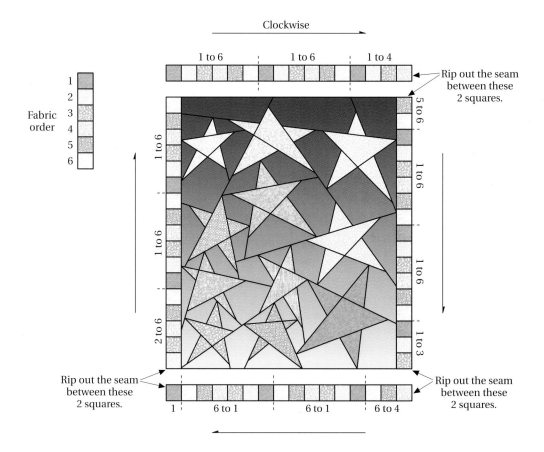

7. Join the segments for each side of the quilt. Sew the inner side borders to the quilt top, then add the inner top and bottom borders; press.

8. Sew the outer side borders to the quilt top; press. Add the outer top and bottom borders, then press the finished quilt top.

9. Referring to "Finishing Techniques" on page 101, prepare a quilt label. Layer the quilt top with batting and backing; baste. Quilt as desired or follow the quilting suggestion. Bind the edges, referring to "Old-Fashioned Binding" on page 108.

Quilting Suggestion

I machine quilted a diamond grid with wavy lines on this quilt, stitching by eye and using a walking foot. After I finished, I realized the quilting pattern looked like a mattress pad! I've provided a diagram of the quilting should you want to follow my lead, but I'm sure you could come up with a more interesting pattern.

WILD GEESE

WILD GEESE *by Shelly Burge, 1995, Lincoln, Nebraska, 16½" x 19½"*

THIS QUILT IS based on the traditional Flying Geese pattern. But these geese must have got into some fermented corn; they are not flying in the usual formation! They are going in every direction and even ricocheting off the borders. Anyone familiar with Caryl Bryer Fallert's work will see her influence in this design.

Foundation paper piecing was the best technique for this quilt because it allowed me to draw every "goose" at a different angle and still piece it easily.

DIMENSIONS: 17" x 20¼"

MATERIALS
❧

- ¼ yd. *total* assorted dark to medium print scraps for geese
- ¼ yd. *total* assorted light print scraps for geese backgrounds
- ⅓ yd. medium print for background and outer border (I used a Hoffman Bali Batik)
- ⅛ yd. dark print for the inner border and binding
- 19" x 23" piece of batting

Cutting

ALL MEASUREMENTS INCLUDE ¼" seam allowances. Trim the seam allowances to ⅛" after each is sewn to reduce bulk. The pattern for Wild Geese is on the pullout.

From the dark print, cut:
- 2 strips, each 1¼" x 40", for the binding
- 2 strips, each 1" x 13¾", for the side inner borders
- 2 strips, each 1" x 11½", for the top and bottom inner borders

Block Assembly

BECAUSE IT'S MADE with the paper-foundation piecing method, the finished quilt will be the mirror image of the pattern.

1. Tape the Wild Geese pullout pattern to a light box or window. Place a large piece of newsprint over it and tape securely. With a draft-ing ruler and mechanical pencil, trace the pattern, including all grain lines, identification letters, and numbers. Cut apart the pattern with paper scissors.

2. Using a reusable-glue stick, adhere the newsprint templates for the background and border pieces to the wrong side of the medium print. Seam allowances are not included in the templates, so leave at least ½" spaces between them. To add seam allowances, align the ¼" mark of a ruler with each side of the paper templates and rotary cut the fabric.

3. Each unit is identified by letter. The units are stitched, then joined to make the block. No seam allowances are included in the paper-foundation templates, so the fabric must extend over the edges to allow for them. When assembling the geese, I try to place the grain lines of the fabric as shown.

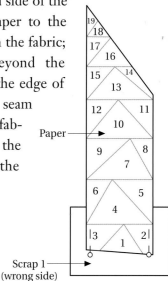

Grain lines in the rows of Wild Geese

Follow this sequence for piecing section H1, then use it as a guide to assemble the other rows of geese. Place a dark scrap for piece 1 right side up on the unmarked side of the paper. Hold the paper to the light as you position the fabric; it must extend beyond the stitching lines and the edge of the paper for the ¼" seam allowances. Pin the fabric in place from the marked side of the paper.

4. Place a light scrap for piece 2 right sides together with scrap 1. Make sure the fabric extends beyond the stitching line for the seam allowance, then pin. Set your sewing machine for a short stitch length, 12 to 13 stitches per inch. Sew on the stitching line, through the paper and both layers of fabric as shown. It isn't necessary to backstitch.

Begin stitching here.

End stitching here.

Scrap 2
(right side)

5. Turn the section over to the fabric side and press scrap 2 back. Check that scrap 2 covers the pattern and extends beyond the edge of the paper for the ¼" seam allowance.

6. Hold the paper out of the way to trim the seam allowance to ⅛". (When piecing the rows of geese, I trimmed each inner seam allowance to ⅛". I left a ¼" seam around the edge of the finished sections, to make joining them easier.)

Paper

Scrap 2

Scrap 1

7. Add a light scrap for piece 3 by repeating steps 4 and 5. Trim the seam allowance when you are done stitching, and press piece 3 back in place.

8. Select a dark scrap for piece 4, and position as shown. Sew on the stitching line. Turn the section over to the fabric side and press scrap 4 back to make sure it is large enough. Trim the seam allowance to ⅛" and press piece 4 back in place.

Stitching line

Scrap 4
(right side)

9. Repeat to finish the section. When you're done, align the ¼" line of a ruler with the edge of the paper and trim the sides of the section with a rotary cutter. Don't remove the paper yet.

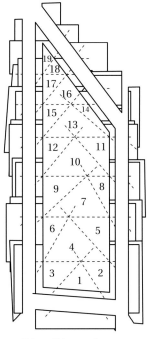

Trim ¼" beyond paper.

10. Piece each row of geese. Note that some rows, such as G4, start with a light background scrap.

11. Refer to the pullout pattern to arrange the pieces paper side up. I use the "pin and poke" method to align the pieces. Put a pin in the corners of each template to line up 2 pieces as shown. Run a pin next to the paper to be sure the template underneath is in the correct position. Stitch right along the edge of the paper.

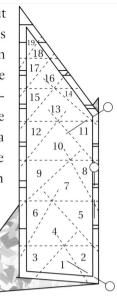

12. Join the pieces for each lettered unit. For example, sew H1 to H2. Add H3 to H1, and press the seam allowances away from the row of geese. Stitch the H4 section in place. Complete all the units.

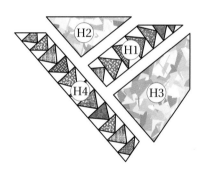

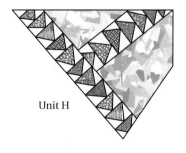

Unit H

13. Sew a partial seam between units A and B, stopping at the dot on the pattern. Sew C to the A-B units. Join the D and E units together. Stitch D-E to C. Add the F unit and then the G unit. Sew the H unit in place, then finish the partial seam between A-H and B to complete the block. Remove the paper and press.

14. Sew the inner side borders to the quilt top. Add the top and bottom inner borders; press.

15. Stitch the top outer border (I) to the quilt top, stopping at the dot on the pattern. Add border unit J to the right side, and sew unit K to the bottom. Add unit L to the left side, then finish the top border seam.

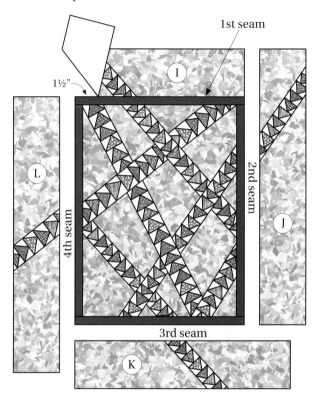

16. Referring to "Finishing Techniques" on page 101, prepare a quilt label. Layer the quilt top with batting and backing; baste. Quilt as desired, or follow the quilting suggestion. Bind the edges to finish.

Design Option

DESIGN YOUR OWN Wild Geese paper-foundation pattern for a quilt or vest:

1. Draft a design on newsprint with a mechanical pencil and drafting ruler. Remember that the finished quilt will be the mirror image of the paper foundation.

Quilting Suggestion

To enhance the ricochet effect of the rows of geese, I used a simple straight-line quilting design. Lay a ruler across the quilt at an angle, and place a strip of masking tape next to it. The ruler ensures that the tape runs straight. Sew along the edge of the tape, stopping the stitches at the inner border and continuing them on the other side. This break in the stitches makes it look as though the quilting passes under the border, just as the rows of geese do. Continue placing the tape at angles over the quilt and sewing along it until you feel there is enough quilting.

2. Draw the outline of the finished dimensions for the quilt or vest pieces. Add the inner and outer borders. Draw lines of the desired width for each row of geese. Decide which rows go over and under each other. Remember: they can also go over or under the inner border.

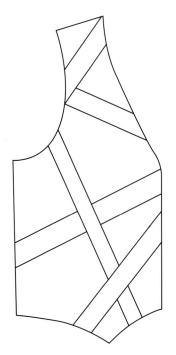

Vest front panel

3. Divide each row into rectangles. The rectangles can be equal in size, or varied.

4. Mark the "nose" of the geese triangles in each of the rectangles. This point can be in the center of the row for a traditional look, or it can vary for a wilder effect. Add 2 lines to connect the "nose" to the opposite corners in each rectangle.

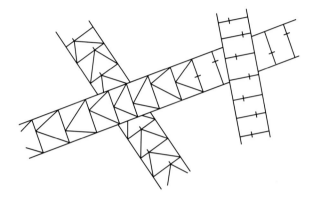

5. Decide on the piecing order and label the sections to complete the paper-foundation pattern. It is important to make a photocopy of the pattern to use as a reference while sewing. Do it *before* you carefully cut the newsprint pattern apart.

Tip

❧

Check at your local newspaper office for inexpensive rolls of newsprint. Rolls are not allowed to run out of paper on the presses, so the printers take the rolls off when they get low. Most newspaper offices sell these paper rolls for a few dollars; some even give them away. The rolls come in various widths.

SPRING TULIPS

SPRING TULIPS *by Shelly Burge, 1994, Lincoln, Nebraska, 22" x 22".*

I**T'S FUN TO** give traditional blocks a little nudge toward something different. That's why this quilt was designed to hang tilted. The blocks have a few surprises, too. A folded square of fabric for the tulip's center point gives it dimension. Also, the Pinwheel blocks are not made with the usual bias squares. They use less dark fabric than traditional blocks for a softer effect.

DIMENSIONS: 22" x 22"

BLOCK SIZE: 3" x 3"

MATERIALS

꙳

- 8 different tie-dyed fabrics, each 5" x 5", for tulips*
- 4 values of green solid squares, each 5" x 5", for leaves
- ½ yd. dark print for the Pinwheel blocks
- ½ yd. very light tan print for the block background
- ⅛ yd. light tan print for the setting pieces
- ¼ yd. medium tan print for the setting pieces
- ¼ yd. dark tan print for the border pieces
- ⅛ yd. darkest tan print for the binding
- ¾ yd. for the backing
- 24" x 24" piece of batting

*I used hand-dyed fabrics with "tie-dyed" dark and light areas in each piece. If you prefer to use prints, you'll need 8 dark print squares, each 4" x 4", and 8 light print squares, each 2" x 2", for the tulips.

Cutting

ALL MEASUREMENTS INCLUDE ¼" seam allowances. The templates for Spring Tulips are on the pullout pattern. Refer to "Templates" on page 8 to prepare rotary-cutting templates.

From *each* of the 8 tie-dyed fabrics, cut:
- 1 square from a dark area, 1⅝" x 1⅝", for tulips (A)
- 1 square from the lightest area, 2" x 2", for tulips (B)
- 1 square from a dark area, 2" x 2"; cut once diagonally to yield 16 triangles for tulips (C)

From *each* of the 4 green solids, cut:
- 2 Template G, to yield 8 leaves
- 2 Template H, to yield 8 leaves

From the dark print, cut:
- 2 angle-cut* strips, each 2" wide, for the Template I pinwheels
- 2 angle-cut* strips, each 2" wide, for the Template J pinwheels

From the very light tan print, cut:
- 1 angle-cut* strip, 2½" wide, for the Template I pinwheels
- 2 angle-cut* strips, each 2" wide, for the Template I pinwheels
- 1 angle-cut* strip, 2½" wide, for the Template J pinwheels
- 2 angle-cut* strips, each 2" wide, for the Template J pinwheels
- 8 squares, each 1⅝" x 1⅝", for the Tulip block (D)
- 8 squares, each 2" x 2"; cut each square once diagonally to yield 16 triangles for the Tulip block (E)
- 8 each of Template F and Template F reversed, for the Tulip block

From the light tan print, cut:
- 5 squares, each 3½" x 3½", for the setting pieces (K)

*Refer to "Angled Cuts" on page 76.

From the medium tan print, cut:
- 3 squares, each 5½" x 5½"; cut each square twice diagonally to yield 12 triangles for the setting pieces (M)
- 4 squares, each 3½" x 3½, for the setting pieces (L)
- 4 squares, each 3" x 3"; cut each square once diagonally to yield 8 triangles for the setting pieces (N)

From the dark tan print, cut:
- 4 Template O, for the border
- 4 Template P, for the border

O P T I O N : *If you want a quilt with square corners, cut 4 Template Q for the border.*

From the darkest tan print, cut:
- 3 strips, each 1¼" x 33", for the binding

Angled Cuts

T H E R E   A R E   6 clockwise and 6 counter-clockwise Pinwheel blocks.

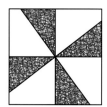

Clockwise Template I

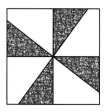

Counter-clockwise Template J

The strips are cut at an angle, so the squares will have straight-grain edges. Use Templates I and J as guides for cutting the correct angles. Notice that the strips are cut at different angles for the two templates.

1. Align a ruler over the templates on the right side of the fabric as shown at right. Remove the template before cutting. To avoid confusion, label the strips I or J. Measure the width of the strip from the cut edge of the fabric.

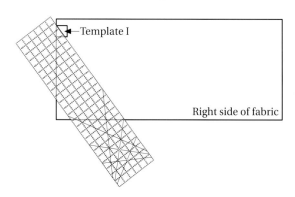

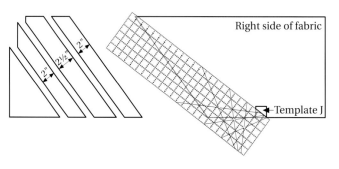

2. Sew together strips for the I unit as shown. Press the seam allowances toward the dark print. Cut 24 Template I squares from the right side of the fabric.

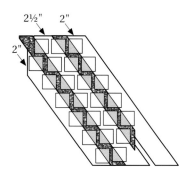

3. Sew together strips for the J unit as shown, then press. Cut 24 Template J squares from the right side of the fabric.

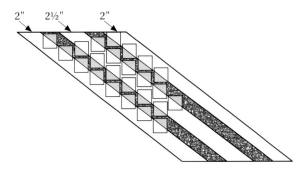

2"   2½"   2"

Block Assembly

1. Fold the B squares in half diagonally, right side out, then fold the corners down to the bottom point as shown.

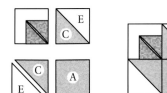

Fold.

Fold corners down.

2. With the folded side out, position B in the corner of the D square and pin in place.

3. Join the pieces of the tulip as shown.

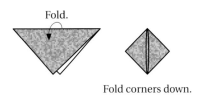

4. Add pieces F and F reversed. Sew on a leaf G, then leaf H to complete the block. Make 8 Tulip blocks.

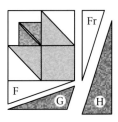

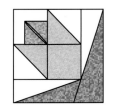

5. Sew 4 I squares together into a Pinwheel block. Make 6 clockwise blocks.

6. Sew 4 J squares together into a Pinwheel block. Make 6 counter-clockwise blocks.

7. Arrange the blocks and setting pieces as shown. Sew into diagonal rows, then join the rows.

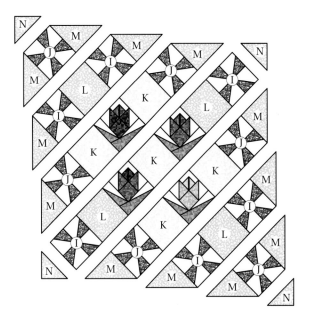

8. The Tulip block is set differently in each border unit; you'll want to keep this in mind as you arrange the blocks. For each border unit, sew piece N to the Tulip block, then add piece O and piece P. Press after each addition.

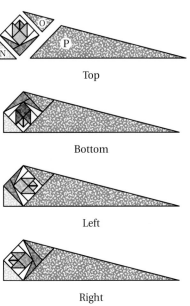

Top

Bottom

Left

Right

9. Sew the top border to the quilt top, stopping the seam 3" from the right edge of the quilt.

10. Sew the left border to the quilt top. Add the bottom border, then the right border. Finish the top border seam.

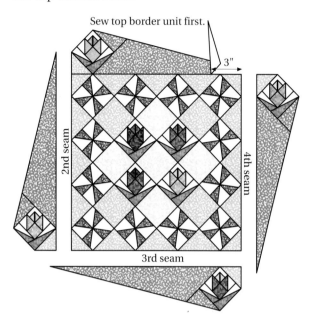

Sew top border unit first.

3"

2nd seam

4th seam

3rd seam

11. If a square quilt is desired, add a piece Q to each corner.

12. Referring to "Finishing Techniques" on page 101, prepare a quilt label. Layer the quilt top with batting and backing; baste. Quilt as desired or follow the quilting suggestion.

Binding

1. The corners of the tulip quilt are *not* 45-degree angles, the angle normally used for mitering. To miter these corners, put a pin in the quilt top, dividing the angle in half. Sew the binding to the quilt top with a ¼" seam allowance, stopping at the pin as shown. Backstitch.

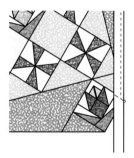

2. Fold the binding over the pin, and hold in place. For the second fold, flip the binding back down and align the edge of the binding with the edge of the quilt. Continue sewing until you stop at the next pin. Complete the binding, mitering each corner as you go.

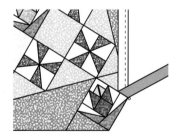

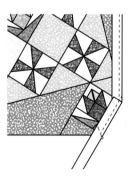

3. Turn the binding over to the back of the quilt. Adjust the folds in each corner as needed. Hand sew the binding to the backing fabric to finish the quilt.

Quilting Suggestion

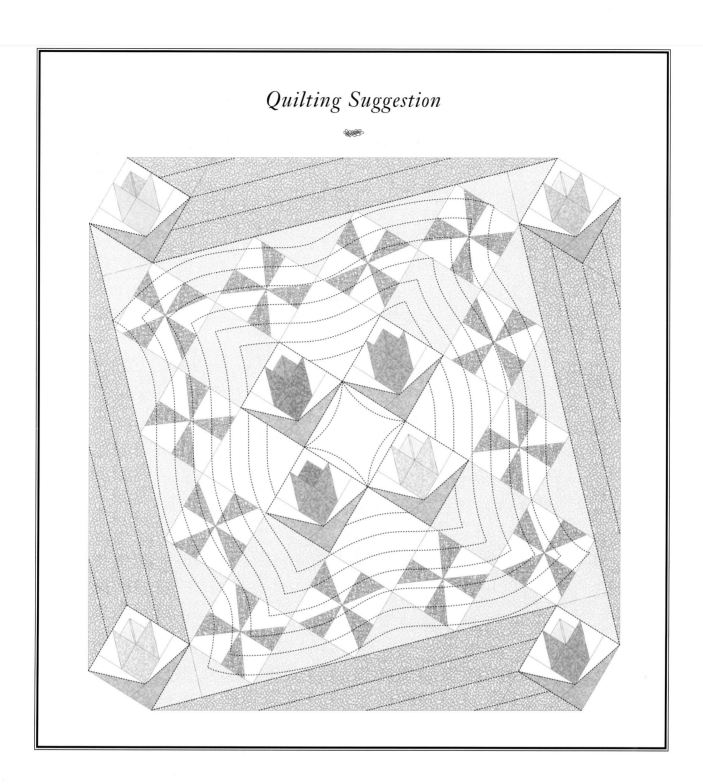

DUST RAG QUILT

DUST RAG QUILT *by Shelly Burge, 1997, Lincoln, Nebraska, 16½" x 16½".*

I THOUGHT THE name of this quilt might get your attention. It's not that I don't like this quilt, but the workmanship isn't the best—promise me you won't look too close. Nebraska quilters have an old saying: "If the quilt looks all right from the back of a galloping horse a half-mile away, it's fine."

This quilt isn't quite that bad, but it was one of those late-night projects. I fixed a big bowl of popcorn, put an old Katharine Hepburn movie into the VCR, dumped the scrap basket on the table, and started cutting squares—I used 108 different prints for the blocks. I figured if I wasn't happy with the quilt top, it would still be a great dust rag. My husband claims this will never happen because I never dust.

DIMENSIONS: 15½" x 15½"
BLOCK SIZE: 1¼" x 1¼"

MATERIALS

❦

- 54 assorted dark print squares, each 2⅛" x 2⅛", for the blocks*
- 54 assorted medium and light print squares, each 2⅛" x 2⅛", for the blocks*
- 1 blue print fat quarter for the inner border
- 1 gold print fat quarter for middle border
- 1 dark blue print fat quarter for the binding
- 1 fat quarter for the backing
- 18" x 18" piece of batting
- Adhesive shelf paper and rubber cement for the quilting template (see page 8)

*Cut accurately; these are exact measurements.

TIP: *I got an idea from an antique quilt on how to achieve a great scrap look. The quilt-maker didn't have enough fabric for all four sides of her border, so she used two fabrics that looked almost the same—a charming surprise when someone takes a close look. For the Dust Rag Quilt, I used two blue prints for the inner border: one for the sides and another for the top and bottom. I used two gold prints for the middle border, again using one for the sides and one for the top and bottom.*

Cutting

ALL MEASUREMENTS INCLUDE ¼" seam allowances.

From the 108 squares:
- Set aside 2 dark and 2 light squares for the outer border corners
- Cut each of the remaining 104 squares once diagonally to yield 208 triangles for the blocks and outer border

From the *lengthwise* grain of the blue print, cut:
- 2 strips, each 1" x 11", for the inner top and bottom borders
- 2 strips, each 1" x 10½", for the inner side borders

From the *lengthwise* grain of the gold print, cut:
- 2 strips, each 1¼" x 13", for the middle top and bottom borders
- 2 strips, each 1¼" x 11½", for the middle side border

From the *lengthwise* grain of the dark blue print, cut:
- 4 strips, each 1¼" x 18", for the binding

Quilt Assembly

1. Sew a dark print triangle to each of the medium and light print triangles to make 104 bias squares, each 1¾" x 1¾" unfinished. Don't sew the same prints together more than once. Press the seam allowances toward the dark print.

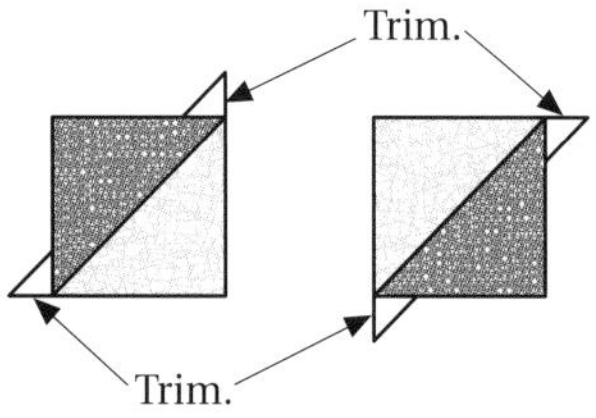

2. Sew 16 bias squares into units as shown. Make 4 units.

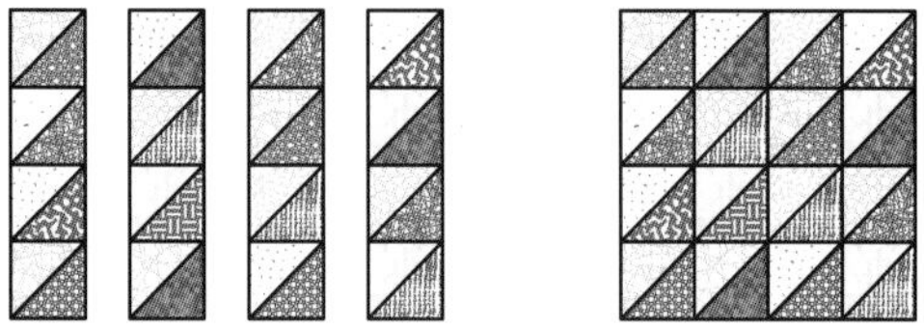

3. Position the 4 units so that all the dark triangles point toward the center. Join the units.

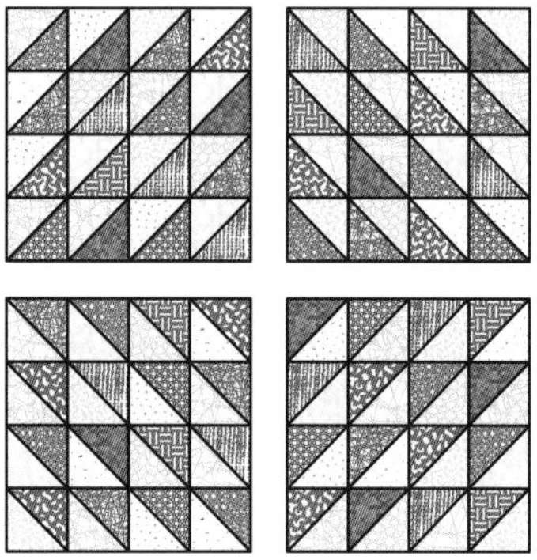

4. Sew the inner side border strips to the quilt top; press. Add the top and bottom inner borders; press.

5. Sew the middle side border strips to the quilt top; press. Add the top and bottom middle borders; press.

6. Arrange the remaining 40 bias squares around the quilt top for the outer pieced border. Sew the bias squares into 4 border sections. Sew the side borders to the quilt. Add the corner squares to the top and bottom borders, then sew the borders to the quilt top; press.

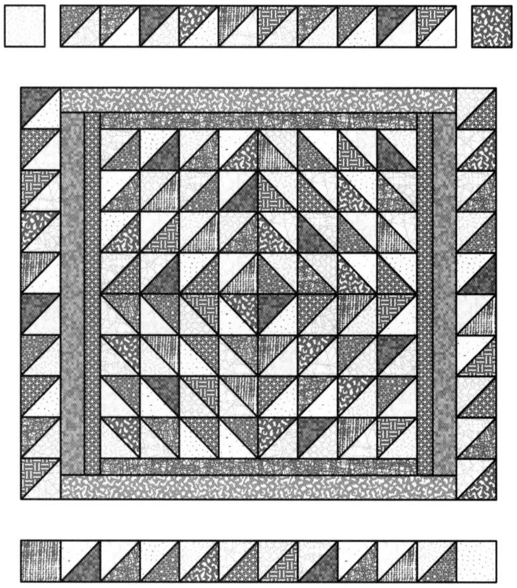

7. Referring to "Finishing Techniques" on page 101, prepare a quilt label. Layer the quilt top with batting and backing; baste. Quilt as desired, or follow the quilting suggestion. Bind the edges to finish.

Tip

To enhance the aged look of this quilt, use two shades of tan thread for the quilting. Alternate colors each time the needle runs out of thread.

Quilting Suggestion

1. Cut a 15½" x 15½" square from newsprint. Fold the square into fourths, then into a triangle as shown.

2. Mark a line 2½" (the width of the 3 borders) from the unfolded edge.

3. Make the template on the pullout pattern. Align the straight edge of the template with the unfolded edge of the paper, then trace the curved edge onto the paper.

4. Cut on the curved line. Unfold the paper, then position it on the quilt to check the fit. If necessary, make adjustments by

refolding and trimming the paper. Do not cut beyond the straight line.

5. Cut the paper pattern into quarters and glue 1 quarter to the back of adhesive shelf paper with rubber cement. Cut out the quilting template, peel off the paper backing, and adhere it to the quilt top. Quilt along the edge of the paper. Reposition the pattern to quilt each quarter of the border.

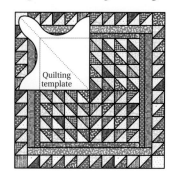

WARM FUZZY HEARTS

WARM FUZZY HEARTS *by Shelly Burge, 1993, Lincoln, Nebraska, 12⅜" x 15⅜".*

Mᴏsᴛ ǫᴜɪʟᴛᴍᴀᴋᴇʀs sᴀᴠᴇ small scraps from their projects to use in other quilts. The major question is, when is a piece of fabric too small to save? For my Confetti Appliqué method, which is a variation of a technique I learned from Jenni Dobson, no piece is too small. Even tiny bits of thread, lace, and silk ribbon can be mixed with the fabric confetti to create fun projects like this heart quilt. Think about the interesting designs you could add to quilts, garments, and decorator items with this method.

DIMENSIONS: 12⅜" x 15⅜"
BLOCK SIZE: 2¼" x 2¼"

MATERIALS

❧

- ¼ yd. *total* assorted dark and medium print scraps for the setting blocks and outer border
- ⅛ yd. black print for the inner border
- 1 black stripe fat quarter for bias binding
- 3 cups assorted small scraps of red, blue, purple, and other fabrics for confetti*
- 6 assorted tan prints, each 3" x 3", for the block backgrounds
- 1 fat quarter for the backing
- 14½" x 17½" piece of batting
- ⅛ yd. of paper-backed fusible web
- Small plastic bags

*The quilt shown has 1 heart each in red, blue, and purple, and 3 hearts in assorted colors. Use whatever scraps you have to make the hearts. Pick fabrics with strong color saturation; don't use prints with light backgrounds. Avoid dark fabrics that are very light on their wrong sides. Combine prints and solids, even thread scraps and frayed edges. I recommend mixing at least 6 or 7 fabrics for each heart.

Cutting

ALL MEASUREMENTS INCLUDE ¼" seam allowances.

From the assorted dark and medium scraps, cut:

- 15 squares, each 1⅝" x 1⅝"; cut each square once diagonally to yield 30 triangles for the setting blocks
- 110" *total* of 1½"-wide strips, each 3" to 5" long, for the middle and outer pieced borders
- 40 squares, each 1¼" x 1¼", for the setting blocks

From the black print, cut:

- 2 strips, each 1¼" x 10¼", for the inner side borders
- 2 strips, each 1¼" x 8½", for the inner top and bottom borders

From the black stripe, cut:

- 3 bias strips, each 1¼" x 22", for the bias binding

From the paper-backed fusible web, cut:

- 6 squares, each 2½" x 2½", for the Confetti Heart blocks

To prepare the confetti from the tiny scraps:

1. Layer 4 to 6 scraps on a cutting mat, 1 color group at a time. Rotary cut across the stack, making cuts approximately ¼" apart. It's not necessary to use a ruler; the cuts don't need to be exact. Turn the mat to make crosscuts perpendicular to the first cuts. Please, be very careful of your fingers while cutting!

2. Cut any remaining scraps of that color into confetti, then stir all the confetti of 1 color together. About 2 tablespoons are needed for each heart. (Don't sneeze, or there will be confetti everywhere.) Store each color separately in small plastic bags.

3. Lay 1 square of fusible web over the template on page 88 and trace the heart outline. Stack all six squares, placing the traced heart on top, then pin. Cut the stack of hearts on the pencil line. Do not add a seam allowance.

Confetti Heart Blocks Assembly

1. Following the fusible-web manufacturer's directions, use an iron to press a heart onto the right side of a 3" tan square as shown.

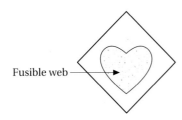

Fusible web

2. Lightly trace around each heart with a pencil. Remove the paper backing, then sprinkle confetti evenly over the heart and outside the pencil lines. The confetti should be about $\frac{1}{16}$" thick.

3. Cover the confetti with a pressing cloth and press. Let the block cool before shaking off the loose pieces. Make sure you leave a good layer of confetti, with no bare spots.

4. Carefully use scissors to trim any confetti that extends beyond the pencil line. Do *not* cut the background fabric.

5. Prepare the sewing machine for free-motion stitching. (If you have never done this type of stitching before, it would be a good idea to make a practice piece.) Cover the heart with meandering stitches. Stitch close to the edge, but don't sew into the background.

TIP: *For the free-motion stitching, pick a cotton thread that blends with the confetti colors. To add sparkle to the hearts, try variegated or metallic thread.*

6. If the confetti shifted over the line during stitching, trim the edge of the heart again. Press the block lightly. Make 6 blocks.

7. Trim the Confetti Heart blocks to 2¾" x 2¾", centering the heart.

TIP: *To ensure that the heart is centered, make a cutting guide. Place a Bias Square ruler over the heart template, positioning the zero in the upper right corner of the template. Tape a paper heart (saved from the fusible web) to the ruler. Place the Bias Square over the Confetti Heart block, positioning the paper heart directly over the confetti heart. Trim 2 sides of the block. Turn the block to trim the other 2 sides so the block measures 2¾" x 2¾".*

Setting Blocks Assemby

1. Make 2 Nine Patch blocks as shown.

2. Make 6 side triangles as shown.

3. Make 4 corner triangles as shown.

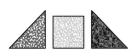

Trim points.

Quilt Top Assembly

1. Arrange the blocks in diagonal rows, then join the rows. Add the corner triangles last.

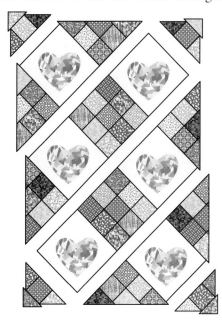

2. Use a rotary cutter and ruler to trim the sides of the quilt, leaving a ¼" seam allowance.

3. Sew the inner side borders to the quilt top; press. Add the inner top and bottom borders; press.

4. Arrange the strips for the middle and outer pieced borders around the quilt top as shown.

5. Cut and join the strips to make the middle and outer borders as follows:

- 2 segments, each 1½" x 12", for the middle side borders
- 2 segments, each 1½" x 10", for the middle top and bottom borders
- 2 segments, each 1½" x 15", for the outer side borders
- 2 segments, each 1½" x 12", for the outer top and bottom borders

6. Sew the top middle border to the quilt top, stopping the stitching 2" from the left side of the quilt. Press and trim the border even with the right side of the quilt.

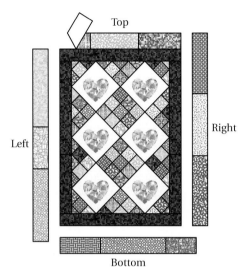

7. Working clockwise, sew the right middle border, the bottom middle border and the left middle border to the quilt top. Press and trim after each addition. Finish the seam of the top middle border and trim.

8. Sew outer-border segments to the quilt top in the same order as for the middle border.

9. Referring to "Finishing Techniques" on page 101, prepare a quilt label. Layer the quilt top with batting and backing; baste. Quilt as desired, or follow the quilting suggestion. Bind the edges to finish.

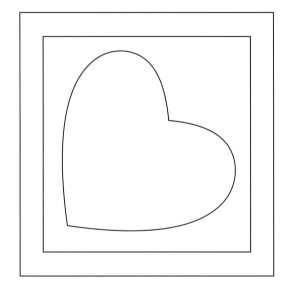

Template for Confetti Heart block
Cut each background square 3" x 3",
then trim to 2¾" x 2¾" after stitching the heart.

Quilting Suggestion

SPIRIT TRAIL

SPIRIT TRAIL *by Shelly Burge, 1991, Lincoln, Nebraska, 36" x 36".*

THIS QUILT WAS inspired by my interest in the history of the Great Plains. It could be made without the silhouettes, but I think they are what sets this quilt apart, along with the four Native American symbols used for the quilting designs. I got the faded antique look by piecing with the light background prints wrong side out.

I love quilts in which blocks connect to become lost in the overall design. When someone says they can't find the block, I know I have achieved my goal.

DIMENSIONS: 36" x 36"
BLOCK SIZE: 4½" x 4½"

MATERIALS

❧

- 1¼ yds. *total* assorted light prints for the blocks
- 1½ yds. *total* assorted dark prints for the blocks
- ⅓ yd. black solid for appliqués and inner border
- 1⅛ yds. for the backing
- 1 skein black embroidery floss
- 38" x 38" piece of batting

Cutting

ALL MEASUREMENTS INCLUDE ¼" seam allowances. Trim the seam allowances to ⅛" after each is sewn to reduce bulk. The templates for Spirit Trail are on the pullout pattern. Refer to "Templates" on page 8 for help in preparing them.

From the *lengthwise* grain of the light prints, cut:

- 12 strips, each 1¼" x 9", for the binding
- 8 strips, each 1¼" x 5½", for the binding
- 30 strips, each 1" x 18", for the Mock Log Cabin blocks
- 36 strips, each 1" x 8", for the String Border blocks
- 1"-wide strips, total 760" in length, for the Courthouse Step blocks

From the *lengthwise* grain of the dark prints, cut:

- 55 strips, each 1" x 18", for the Mock Log Cabin blocks
- 16 rectangles, each 1" x 1¼", for the binding
- 1"-wide strips, total 940" in length, for the Courthouse Step blocks

From the *lengthwise* grain of the black solid, cut:

- 12 strips, each 1" x 5", for the String Border blocks
- 8 strips, each 1" x 3¾", for the Corner blocks

Mock Log Cabin Block Assembly

1. To make a strip unit, sew five 18"-long light strips together, offsetting the ends by ½" as shown below. Make 6 strip units.

2. Cut 6 Template A from each strip unit to yield 36 triangles. Place the template guidelines over the seam lines when cutting.

Template A

3. Join 4 triangles, cut from 4 different light strip units, to make a light Mock Log Cabin block as shown. The pressing direction of the seam allowances should alternate from triangle to triangle. Make 9 light Mock Log Cabin blocks.

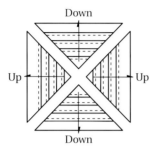

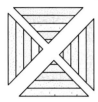

Light Mock Log Cabin

4. Sew five 18"-long dark strips together as you did for the light strips. Make 11 strip units.

5. Cut 6 Template A triangles from each strip unit to yield 66 triangles (64 needed for the blocks).

6. Join 4 dark triangles into a block, alternating the pressing direction of the seam allowances. Make 16 dark Mock Log Cabin blocks.

Dark Mock Log Cabin

Courthouse Step Block Assembly

THE COURTHOUSE STEP blocks are sewn with the Stitch and Trim technique, using the 1"-wide strips.

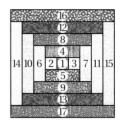

1. From a 1"-wide dark print strip, cut a 1" x 1" square for the block center (1).

2. Sew 2 light strips (2 & 3) to opposite sides of the square, then press. (Press all seam allowances away from the center square.) Use a rotary cutter and ruler to trim the block as shown.

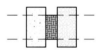

3. Add 2 dark strips (4 & 5) as shown. Press and trim.

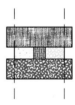

4. Add 2 light strips (6 & 7). Press and trim.

5. Add 2 dark strips (8 & 9). Press and trim.

6. Add 2 light strips (10 & 11). Press and trim.

7. Add 2 dark strips (12 & 13). Press and trim.

8. Add 2 light strips (14 & 15). Press and trim.

9. Stitch the last 2 dark strips (16 & 17). Press and trim to finish the block. Make 24 Courthouse Step blocks. Using a Bias Square ruler, check to be sure the blocks are square.

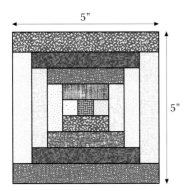

5"

5"

Courthouse Step Block

Courthouse Step Half-Block Assembly

USE THE 1"-wide strips to piece the half-blocks, using the same technique as for the full Courthouse Step blocks. Stitch the half-blocks in the order shown. Make 16.

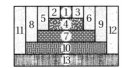

Courthouse Step Half-block

String Border Block Assembly

1. Join nine 1" x 8" light strips as shown. Cut the strip unit into 3 segments, each 2½" wide. Make 4 strip units to yield 12 segments.

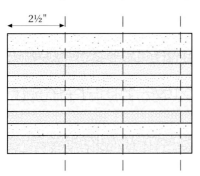

2½"

2. Sew a 1" x 5" black strip to the bottom of each segment.

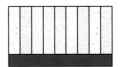

String Border Block

Corner Block Assembly

1. Using one 1" x 3¾" black strip and 4 left-over 1"-wide light strips for each unit, make 4 strip-pieced units and 4 reversed units. Place the black strip at the bottom of each unit, and make sure the light strips are long enough to accommodate Template B. Cut 4 Template B and 4 Template B reversed.

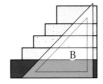

2. Make 4 corner blocks by joining 1 piece B and 1 piece B reversed for each.

Corner Block

Quilt Top Assembly

1. Arrange the blocks, alternating the direction of the Courthouse Step blocks in every other row. Take care: the same fabrics should not touch.

2. Sew the blocks into segments as shown. Join the segments.

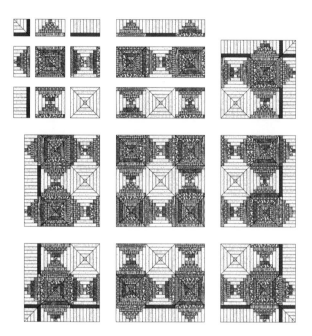

Appliqué Silhouettes

1. Referring to "Freezer-Paper Appliqué" on page 98, use the silhouette templates on the pullout to prepare the appliqué pieces. Position the pieces one at a time on the light fabric areas and hand appliqué in place with black thread. Carefully trim the background fabric behind each appliqué and remove the paper. The antlers on the antelope and elk are very narrow, so I did not remove the freezer paper from those areas. Use a double strand of black embroidery thread to hand stitch the reins and tail tie on the horse.

2. Referring to "Finishing Techniques" on page 101, prepare a quilt label. Layer the quilt top with batting and backing; baste. Quilt as desired, or follow the quilting suggestion.

Binding

REFERRING TO "Old-Fashioned Binding" on page 108, piece 4 binding units as shown. Sew them to the quilt top, matching the dark squares of each binding unit to the dark squares of the Courthouse Step half-blocks.

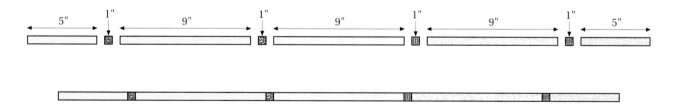

NOTE: *Rather than appliqué the five silhouette designs, you could outline-quilt them with black thread.*

Quilting Suggestion

I STITCHED THE four quilting patterns with black thread. They are traditional Plains tribe designs often done in bead or quillwork. It was important for me to know the meanings of the symbols, and I thought it might interest you also.

Peace Star: All directions come together in harmony at the center of this design. Their meeting stops conflict and creates peace.

Medicine Wheel: The hoop represents the never-ending circle of life. It is divided by four bars, which represent the four directions and all creation. The West represents danger, the North life, the East knowledge, and the South quiet.

Iktomi, the Spider People: This may be the oldest of all Lakota designs. The symbol represents the legend of the Spider People. The Creator instructed these spiritual beings to teach the first people how to live with nature. The four points in the design represent the four directions.

Shooting Star: The starburst is an early Sioux design that provides protection from danger. It represents the spiritual and physical powers of the sun and the stars, the sky beings.

THE FRAMED FINISH

THIS IS A great gift idea and a quick way to finish a project. Check out the wonderful frame styles available at discount and hobby stores. You could use antique frames or even garage-sale finds for this technique. Craft and hobby shops stock mat boards in dozens of colors. Acid-free mats are also available.

Assembling the Framed Block

1. Choose a block pattern: there are several in the Zigzag Sampler on page 17. Follow the instructions to assemble the block.

2. Purchase an uncut mat board in a color that complements the fabrics in the block. You can cut the mat to size with a rotary cutter. Select a frame with glass, as well as cardboard for the back.

3. Referring to "Batting" on page 103, cut a square of thin batting ⅛" smaller than the unfinished block. Trim any frayed threads from the raw edges of the block and put strips of double-stick tape on the back of the block, as shown. Center the batting over the block. Apply strips of double-stick tape to the edges of the batting.

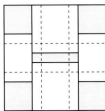 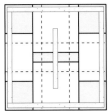

Back of the block   Double-stick tape on the back

4. Carefully position the block on the right side of the mat and gently press it in place with your fingers. Place the glass and the matted block into the frame, secure, and attach a saw-tooth hanger.

Options

• Select a small frame to fit the size of the finished block. It will not need a mat.

• Piece a small quilt top, then frame it unquilted.

• To frame a quilted piece, I recommend stitching the quilt to the mat. With a large, sharp needle and pliers, punch a grid of holes through the mat. (The holes will be covered by the quilt.) Use a needle and thread to sew through these holes and make a small tack stitch in the quilt, then go back through the next hole. Purchase spacers to put in the frame between the glass and the mat board to prevent the glass from crushing the quilt.

ANTIQUE FABRICS

ONE OF MY favorite pastimes is browsing through antique malls, flea markets, and garage sales. I'm always looking for toy sewing machines to add to my collection, as well as antique fabric. Finding a French toile or beautiful indigo print is a fabric-lover's dream come true. I can't pass up a chance to dig through boxes of odds and ends in search of buried treasure. I select fabrics that are sturdy and in good condition, but holes and stains don't worry me because I can cut around them. Unfinished quilt blocks are a good source of fabrics, too.

Making small quilts from old fabrics is a great way to put your fabric collection on display for everyone to enjoy. Older materials may not be as durable as new ones, but they will be fine in a small wall hanging.

Indigo blues, maroons, and mourning gray prints are my favorites. It can be difficult to find large pieces to use for setting blocks, borders, and bindings. For that reason, I look for new fabrics that blend with the old. With the variety of reproduction prints currently on the market, that's not too difficult.

I use rotary-cutting techniques with antique fabrics. However, it's difficult to use strip-piecing methods because the pieces are usually small.

Care and Storage

KEEP ANTIQUE FABRICS in sealed plastic bags until they can be washed, as a precaution against insects. Old fabrics may look clean, but they are usually full of dust. Before they go in a quilt, I want to be sure the fabrics are completely clean and the dye is set.

To wash vintage fabrics, first separate by color. Large pieces—half-yard cuts or more—can be washed in the machine on the delicate cycle. Wash smaller pieces in the sink with warm water and a mild detergent, such as Orvus. Gently swish the fabrics in the water by hand. If the water looks very dirty, drain and rinse the sink, then refill it with soapy water. Rinse the fabric several times with clear water to completely remove the soap. In the last rinse, add a 4" square of muslin to check for bleeding. If the muslin changes color, keep rinsing, then check again with a new square. Dry the fabric indoors, on a clothesline or spread on a towel. Press the fabric and store it in a clear plastic box.

Laundering vintage fabric is a good way to test how strong it is. I'd rather have a fabric fall apart in the wash than have it disintegrate in a finished quilt.

Backing Fabric

When I make a small quilt with antique fabrics, I like to continue the vintage look by using old flour and sugar sacks for the backing. Sack backings are a nice way to preserve textiles and carry on the tradition found in many early quilts.

Old flour sacks can be used for the front of the quilt as well, as shown on page 63. I wash the sacks as described on page 97.

❧ FREEZER-PAPER APPLIQUÉ

THE APPLIQUÉ METHOD I prefer combines freezer-paper templates with Quilter's GluTube. This technique allows me to create detailed designs. Remember: the paper goes on the wrong side of the fabric. The finished appliqué will be the *mirror image* of the pattern.

1.   With a pencil, trace the appliqué design onto the dull side of the freezer paper—if necessary, place the pattern and freezer paper on a light box or against a window. Trace the pattern, including grain lines and template numbers. Cut out the template on the pencil line with paper

scissors (no seam allowances are needed). Use a paper punch to make a hole in the center of each template.

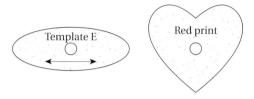

2.   Place the templates shiny-side down on the wrong side of the fabric. Seam allowances are not included in the template, so leave space to add them when you cut. On a firm ironing surface, press with a dry iron at the highest setting.

3.   Using a Quilter's GluTube, apply a generous ⅛"-wide band of glue to both the template and the fabric. Let the glue dry for a moment before you cut out the pieces. Add a generous ⅛" seam allowance by eye as you cut.

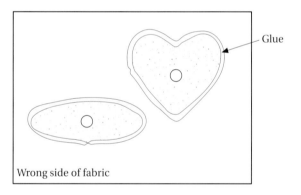

4.   Clip the curves, then carefully fold the seam allowance over the edge of the template. Work the fabric to get smooth, clean edges. The fabric can be pulled up and repositioned. Do not use an iron.

Clip curves.

5. When the appliqué pieces are ready, position them on the background fabric and pin in place. If one appliqué piece overlaps another, start with the bottom layer and work your way up. Hand stitch with thread that matches the appliqué piece.

6. After the stitching is finished, carefully cut a slit in the background fabric behind each appliqué. Trim the background, leaving a ¼" seam allowance. (The paper helps keep you from cutting through to the front of the quilt.) Run a small crochet hook or another long tool with a dull point through the hole in the template. Slide the crochet hook around to separate the freezer paper from the fabric, then gently pull out the paper. Use tweezers to remove paper from small areas.

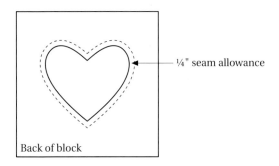

¼" seam allowance

Back of block

The black silhouettes in Spirit Trail on page 90 were done with this technique. I don't think it would have been possible to appliqué the elk antlers with any other method. I removed the freezer paper from the body of the elk, but the antlers were so narrow that I left the paper in them.

Tip

You could use a fabric gluestick to adhere the seam allowance to the template. To remove the freezer paper, wet the fabric to release the glue.

❧ BORDERS

CREATING THE RIGHT border for your quilt is a delicate balance. A good border should enhance and frame the quilt blocks without overpowering them. I like to audition possible border fabrics by combining them with the assembled quilt blocks on a flannel board. This allows me to look at a variety of prints and colors, adjust widths, and try multiple borders before I start cutting.

For the quilts in this book, I recommend cutting each border strip about 2" longer than required, then trimming to the correct measurement after the blocks are joined. I've given exact cutting measurements for these projects, but if your blocks finish larger than the measurements given in the quilt plan, the border strips won't be long enough.

Grain Lines

I PREFER TO cut borders from the lengthwise grain because it doesn't stretch. I believe this contributes to an accurate quilt that lies flat. The crosswise grain does stretch a little, which might cause waves in the borders. Handle crosswise-grain borders carefully while sewing.

The reason most of the patterns in this book call for crosswise-grain borders is that they require less yardage than lengthwise-grain borders. If you would prefer lengthwise-grain borders for a project that calls for crosswise-grain borders, you'll need more border fabric than is called for in the materials list.

Square Corners

1.   Measure the length of the quilt through the center. Cut the side border pieces to that measurement. Fold the quilt and border strips in half to find the centers, and mark with a pin. Matching the centers and the ends, pin the borders to the quilt top, easing if necessary. Sew with a ¼" seam allowance, then press the seams toward the border.

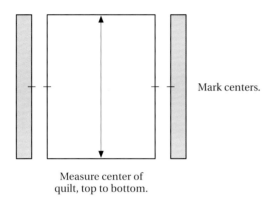

Measure center of
quilt, top to bottom.

Mark centers.

2.   Measure the width of the quilt, including the side borders, through the center. Use that measurement to cut the top and bottom borders. Fold the quilt and border strips in half to find the centers, and mark with a pin. Matching the centers and the ends, pin the borders to the quilt top, easing if necessary. Sew with a ¼" seam allowance, then press the seams toward the borders.

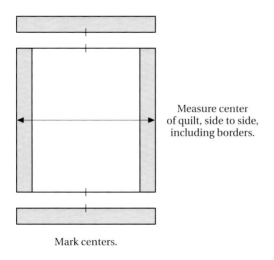

Measure center
of quilt, side to side,
including borders.

Mark centers.

Mitered Corners

1.   Measure the length and width of the quilt top through the center. Record the measurements. To the length measurement, add twice the width of the border strip, plus 2". Cut the side borders to that length. To the quilt width measurement, add twice the width of the border strip, plus 2". Cut the top and bottom borders to that length.

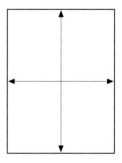

Measure through the center.

2.   For a quilt with 2 or more borders, cut each strip to the length measurement found in step 1. Sew the strips into border units for each side of the quilt. Press the seams in the side borders toward the outer border, and the seams in the top and bottom borders toward the inner border. Wherever the seams meet at the corners, they will lie in opposite directions.

Combine border strips before sewing them to the quilt top.

3.   Fold the quilt and borders in half to find the centers, and mark with pins. Place 2 pins in the side borders to mark the length of the quilt. Place 2 pins in the top and bottom borders to mark the width of the quilt.

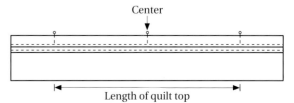

Center

Length of quilt top

4. Pin the side borders to the quilt, matching the centers and the pins in the border with the ends of the quilt. Starting and stopping ¼" from the top and bottom edges of the quilt, sew the border to the quilt with a ¼" seam allowance; backstitch. Press toward the borders.

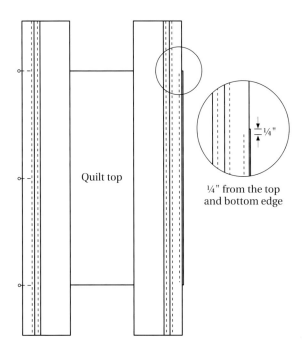

5. Add the top and bottom borders to the quilt top, as mentioned in step 4.

6. Place the first corner to be mitered on your ironing surface, right side up. Lay 1 border strip straight and fold 1 strip back at a 45-degree angle. If the border strips are pieced, make sure the seams align perfectly. Press and pin.

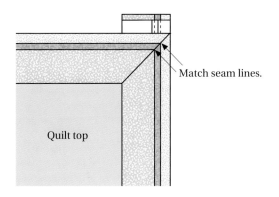

7. Fold the quilt diagonally, right sides together. Match the sides of the borders and pin. Start in the corner and stitch along the pressed crease toward the outside edge.

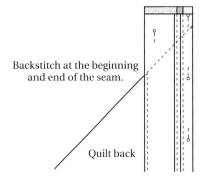

8. Trim the border strips, leaving a ¼" seam allowance. Press the seam to one side. Miter the other corners, using the same process.

FINISHING TECHNIQUES

Labels

THE IDENTIFICATION LABEL is an important part of the quilt; it shouldn't be left to the end as an afterthought. A label provides valuable information for future generations of your family and historians. After all, when your great-great-granddaughter is president of Jupiter, people will want to know her great-great-grandparent made a quilt.

1. Labels can be any shape, including circles, squares, fish, or stars. Select a light solid or a muted tone-on-tone print fabric. Cut a piece of freezer paper the desired size and shape. Draw dark parallel lines on the dull side with a black marker (so it looks like a writing tablet). Iron the freezer paper, shiny side down, to the wrong side of the fabric—the freezer paper stabilizes the

fabric to make writing easier. The dark lines show through the fabric; use them as a guide to keep your handwriting from slanting uphill.

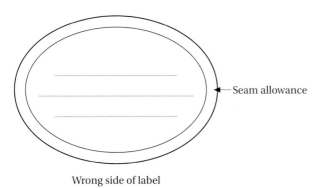

Wrong side of label

2. The label should include the quilt title, your full name and address, the date the quilt was completed, and any other information you want to remember, such as where a special fabric was purchased or what inspired the quilt. Use permanent fabric pens. I prefer ball-point Gelly Roll pens by Sakura.

Give the label some personality. Draw designs that complement the quilt pattern, write each word in a different color, or trace around your child's hand. Use rubber stamps or decorative machine stitches to create a label as unique as your quilt.

When the label is finished, press it to heat set the ink.

3. Refer to "Freezer-Paper Appliqué" on page 98. Turn under the seam allowance as directed. Place the label near the lower right-hand corner of the backing fabric. Remember: the backing is cut larger than the quilt top. Don't put the label too close to the edge. Hand appliqué, then trim the backing fabric behind the label, leaving a ¼" seam.

4. Layer the quilt top, batting, and backing together, making sure the label is at the bottom of the quilt. Baste the layers and quilt by hand or machine, quilting the label along with the quilt top and backing (this makes the label difficult to remove).

Tip

❧

Have you made an incredibly beautiful label and feel quilting stitches would mar it? There is another option. Make a small fabric label with your full name and address. Appliqué it to the backing fabric, then baste and quilt as described in step 4. When the quilt is finished, hand appliqué the beautiful label to the back of the quilt, covering the small label. If the larger label is ever removed, the small label will still be there, quilted into the quilt along with your name and address.

Batting

SCALE THE THICKNESS of the batting to the size of the quilt. A puffy batting could make your small quilt look more like a pillow. I prefer a thin batting with enough loft to show off the quilting stitches. The batting I use most often is Hobbs Thermore, a polyester batting that works beautifully in small quilts and garments. I have never seen it beard or pill. If you prefer cotton batting, Fairfield Soft Touch is nice for small quilts.

Batting scraps trimmed from larger projects can be recycled for small quilts. If your scrap of polyester batting is too thick, you can separate the top and bottom layers, scoop out some of the filling in the middle (sort of like an Oreo cookie), then put the two layers back together.

Cut the batting approximately 2" larger than the quilt top, to allow for shifting while quilting and binding.

Spoon Basting

BASTE YOUR QUILT to prepare it for hand or machine quilting. For simple machine quilting, I use small nickel-plated safety pins to hold the layers together. For a project that will be hand quilted or done with detailed machine quilting, I prefer to hand baste. Always use white or cream-colored thread for basting; dye can bleed from thread, just like it does from fabric. It would be terrible to find dark lines across your quilt top.

Hand basting takes more time than pin basting, but it's worth the extra effort to make sure the layers of the quilt won't shift. There won't be pins in the way, either, to catch during machine quilting or get in the way when you're using a hoop.

1. Find a table, countertop, or floor that has enough space to spread the quilt flat. Pins and needles could leave scratch marks, so don't spread the quilt on valuable furniture.

2. Place the backing fabric on your work surface, wrong side up. The fabric should be free of wrinkles. Use short pieces of masking tape and follow the sequence shown below to tape the fabric to your work surface. Work you way from the middle of each side out to the corners, and alternate from one side to another. The fabric should be stretched slightly. Use a lint brush to remove threads and pet hair before you proceed.

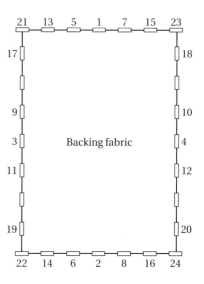

3. Smooth the batting in place and center the quilt top over it. Using straight pins, pin through the 3 layers on all 4 sides, following the sequence shown above. The quilt top should be square and slightly taut.

4. You will need white thread, an embroidery needle, a thimble, and a teaspoon—I buy old spoons at garage sales for basting. Cut a length of thread that is one-and-a-half times the height of the quilt (never knot the thread when basting). In the center of the quilt, take 1 stitch and pull the thread to divide it in half. Baste toward position 1 with stitches that are approximately ¾" long.

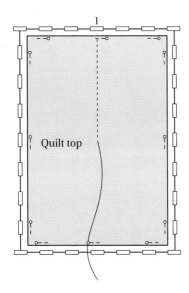

6. At the quilt edge, anchor the thread with a couple of short stitches. Return to the center and rethread the needle with the second half of the thread. Stitch toward position 2, and anchor the thread with short stitches. Cut another thread that is one-and-a-half times the width of the quilt. Start in the center and stitch toward position 3. Rethread the needle and baste to position 4. Continue basting, starting each line of stitches in the middle and rethreading to finish the other half. The basting lines should be about 3" apart.

7. When you are done basting the middle of the quilt, baste ⅛" from the edges. These stitches won't have to be removed, because the binding will cover them.

8. Remove the pins and masking tape, and you are ready to start quilting.

5. Rest the spoon on the quilt. As you baste, bring the needle up through the fabric into the tip of the spoon. Push the needle through while rocking the spoon back, and the needle will point up. This makes it easy to grasp the needle.

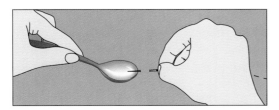

Catch the tip of the needle in the spoon.

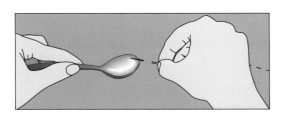

Rock the spoon back as you push the needle through.

Basted quilt

9. After you've finished quilting, clip and pull out the basting threads a few stitches at a time. If a quilting stitch goes through the basting thread, clip the basting thread close to the quilting thread. Fray the end of the basting thread and gently pull it out.

Quilting

CHOOSING THE QUILTING design is usually the hardest part for me, I can debate for days, trying to make up my mind. My favorite quilting patterns for small quilts are overall designs, such as Clamshells, Fans, and Hanging Diamonds. I prefer quilting that flows over the pieced pattern of the quilt, rather than outlining the patchwork. Overall quilt patterns break up the light across the quilt surface in interesting ways to keep the eye moving.

A quilting suggestion has been included for each quilt project. Look through all the quilting designs before choosing one for your quilt. You may prefer a pattern shown with another project.

Marking Patterns

WHEN I STARTED making quilts in 1973, the one thing I disliked was marking the quilt top. Going to all the work of tracing the pattern on the quilt, then having to take it off again, seemed like a waste of time. (Sort of like making beds!) I also had concerns about whether the marking pens would wash out. So I avoided marking quilting patterns as much as possible.

Masking tape is one method I use as a guide for quilting, but it only works for straight lines. When I tried to cut the tape into other shapes, it stuck to the scissors. So I tried adhesive shelf-lining paper, the kind that has a peel-off paper back. This has worked the best for me. To make a quilting template from adhesive shelf paper, cut a design from the paper, peel off the back, and stick the shape on the quilt top. Hand or machine quilt around the template. When one spot is finished, pull up the template and move it

to another area. When the shelf-paper template won't stick any more, cut out another one and continue.

One note of caution about masking tape and shelf paper—they can leave a gummy residue if left on the fabrics for an extended time. To avoid this possibility, don't leave them on the quilt when you are not quilting. The entire top cannot be marked at once if you plan to use masking tape or shelf paper. Mark one line of quilting at a time.

Tip

❦

Buy solid-colored shelf paper; busy prints could strain your eyes.

Backing Fabrics

FOR BACKINGS, I like to use interesting fabrics that contribute to the overall look of the finished quilt. The backing should fit with the theme of the quilt top.

If you use a print for your backing fabric, it might even provide inspiration for the quilting pattern. For Zigzag Sampler on page 17, I quilted over the printed lines on the backing fabric. These lines formed a design similar to the Clamshell quilting pattern.

Back of Zigzag Sampler, page 17

Another example

Thread

WHETHER QUILTING BY hand or machine, select a thread in proportion to the size of the quilt. A heavy quilting thread meant for a full-sized piece would not be appropriate for a small project. Remember: small quilts don't have to survive the wear and tear that a bed quilt would, so a fine thread won't cause problems.

The thread I use most often for machine quilting is DMC Machine Embroidery thread #50. It comes in a nice selection of colors, including several variegated shades.

For hand quilting, I prefer 100% cotton sewing thread if it's available in the color I need. If I can't find 100% cotton thread, I use high quality all-purpose mercerized cotton-covered polyester thread. Hand-quilting stitches should be as small as possible, to be in proportion to the quilt. My best tip for makers of miniature quilts: use a fine thread for hand quilting and it will be easier to achieve small stitches.

Binding

THE BINDING CAN make or break the look of a quilt, so take care to do it well. As I've stressed throughout, everything should be in proportion for small quilts, and that includes the binding. A double-fold binding, also known as a French binding, would create a bulky speed bump on the edge of a little quilt. Bias binding wears better than binding cut from the straight of grain, but the wear factor isn't a concern with small quilts.

I prefer binding cut from the lengthwise grain because it doesn't stretch. The crosswise grain will give a little, which might cause ripples; handle crosswise-grain binding carefully while sewing it to the quilt. Less yardage is required to cut binding from the crosswise grain; for that reason, most of the quilt projects in this book call for crosswise-grain binding. If you prefer lengthwise binding, you'll need more binding fabric than called for in the materials list. An extra ¾ yard would do the trick, letting you cut long, seamless pieces for the binding, with plenty of leftover fabric for another project.

Single Fold

1. To prepare the quilt for binding, machine baste ⅛" from the raw edges of the quilt top on all 4 sides. Use a rotary cutter and ruler to trim excess batting and backing fabric. As you trim the quilt, check the corners to be sure they are 90-degree angles.

2. Cut several strips, each 1¼" wide, and sew them together to make enough binding to go around the quilt. Join the strips at a 45-degree angle. Press the seams to one side.

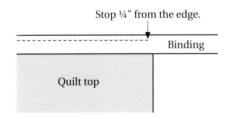

3. Machine stitch the binding to the front of the quilt with a ¼" seam allowance, leaving about 3" of the binding free at the start. To miter the corner, stop and backstitch ¼" from the edge of the quilt top.

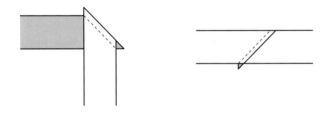

Stop ¼" from the edge.

Binding

Quilt top

4. Fold the binding up at a 45-degree angle, as shown. The fold should meet the corner of the quilt. Fold the binding back down over the 45-degree angle. The second fold should be even with the edge of the quilt. Match the raw edges and sew a ¼" seam along the next side. Repeat these steps at each corner.

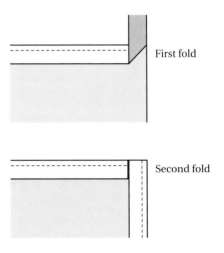

First fold

Second fold

5. Stop sewing 6" from the starting point. Trim the ends of the binding at a 45-degree angle, overlapping the ends ½". Join the ends with a ¼" seam. Finish attaching the binding to the quilt.

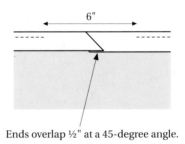

6"

Ends overlap ½" at a 45-degree angle.

6. Turn the edge of the binding under ¼" and fold it to the back of the quilt. Miter the corners, as shown.

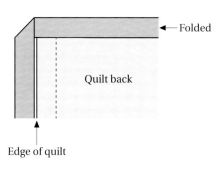

Folded

Quilt back

Edge of quilt

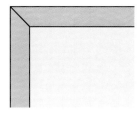

7. On a small quilt, I pin the binding in place all the way around the edge of the quilt before starting the hand stitching. Select a thread color that matches the binding. Blindstitch the binding to the quilt back. Sew the folds in the mitered corners too.

Old-Fashioned Binding

This type of binding probably has an official name, but "Old-Fashioned Binding" is what I call it.

1. Cut 4 strips, each 1¼" wide, for each side of the quilt. Cut the 2 side strips 1" longer than the length of the quilt, and the top and bottom strips 1" longer than the width. Baste and trim the edge of the quilt as directed for Single-Fold Binding. Sew the side strips to the front of the quilt with a ¼" seam allowance. Trim the strips even with the top and bottom of the quilt. Turn the edge of the binding under ¼", fold it to the

back, and pin. Blindstitch the binding to the quilt back.

Quilt back

2. Center the top and bottom binding strips, with an equal amount of fabric extending beyond each side of the quilt. Sew the binding to the quilt with ¼" seams. Trim the ends of the bindings, leaving a ¼" seam allowance.

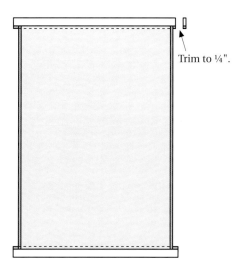

Trim to ¼".

3. This binding can get bulky in the corners because there are so many layers. Trim some of the excess batting and fabric with small scissors. Fold in the ends of the binding, then turn the length of the binding under ¼" and fold it to the back of the quilt.

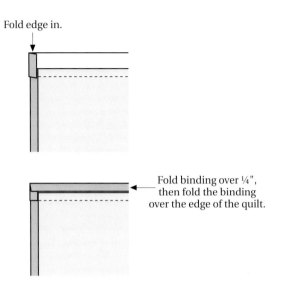

Fold edge in.

Fold binding over ¼", then fold the binding over the edge of the quilt.

4. Pin the top and bottom binding strips in place and hand stitch them to the quilt back. Stitch the fold at the ends of the binding.

Congratulations! I hope you are proud of your accomplishment. Think about hanging it on the wall or draping it over a baby buggy, or maybe entering the next quilt show? I hope to see it, and you, there.

RESOURCES

Cherrywood Fabrics

PO Box 486
Brainerd, MN 56401-0486
(218) 829-0967
Suede-look hand-dyed fabrics

Country House Cottons

PO Box 375
Fayette, IA 52142
(319) 425-4384
Handdyed@aol.com
Hand-dyed fabrics

Flynn Quilt Frame Company

1000 Shiloh Overpass Road
Billings, MT 59106
(800) 745-3596
www.flynnquilt.com
Template material

The Kirk Collection

1513 Military Avenue
Omaha, NE 68111-3924
(800) 398-2542
www.kirkcollection.com
Antique and quality reproduction fabrics

ABOUT THE AUTHOR

SHELLY BURGE learned to sew when she was four years old but did not become interested in quilting until she was an adult. She began teaching ten years after she learned to quilt and was soon traveling to guilds and conferences nationwide.

In 1977 Shelly started entering quilts in the Nebraska State Fair, where her work has received more than one hundred ribbons, including four Pride of Nebraska awards. Numerous quilting magazines and books have featured her work, and her quilts have won prestigious recognition in national and international quilt and art competitions across the United States, Europe, and Japan.

Shelly promotes the art of quilting. She was one of the founding members of the Nebraska State Quilt Guild, has served on the Nebraska Quilt History Project committee, and is currently volunteering at the International Quilt Study Center based at the University of Nebraska. In addition to *Small Quilts Made Easy*, Shelly is the author of the book *Terrific Triangles*.

In 1992 Shelly was named the first recipient of the Jewel Pearce Patterson Scholarship, sponsored by the International Quilt Association. One American quilting teacher is selected annually for this scholarship. Shelly traveled to Quilt Expo Europa in The Netherlands for her award. At the 1993 Houston International Quilt Festival she curated a display of quilts inspired by that experience.

Shelly and her husband, Clint, live in the home they built outside Lincoln, Nebraska. They have two grown children.

Books from Martingale & Company

FIBER STUDIO PRESS

Appliqué

Appliquilt® Your ABCs
Appliquilt® to Go
Baltimore Bouquets
Basic Quiltmaking Techniques for Hand Appliqué
Coxcomb Quilt
The Easy Art of Appliqué
Folk Art Animals
From a Quilter's Garden
Stars in the Garden
Sunbonnet Sue All Through the Year
Traditional Blocks Meet Appliqué
Welcome to the North Pole

Borders and Bindings

Borders by Design
The Border Workbook
A Fine Finish
Happy Endings
Interlacing Borders
Traditional Quilts with Painless Borders

Design Reference

All New! Copy Art for Quilters
Blockbender Quilts
Color: The Quilter's Guide
Design Essentials: The Quilter's Guide
Design Your Own Quilts
Fine Art Quilts
Freedom in Design
The Log Cabin Design Workbook
Mirror Manipulations
The Nature of Design
QuiltSkills
Sensational Settings
Surprising Designs from Traditional Quilt Blocks
Whimsies & Whynots

Foundation/Paper Piecing

Classic Quilts with Precise Foundation Piecing
Crazy but Pieceable
Easy Machine Paper Piecing
Easy Mix & Match Machine Paper Piecing
Easy Paper-Pieced Keepsake Quilts
Easy Paper-Pieced Miniatures
Easy Reversible Vests
Go Wild with Quilts
Go Wild with Quilts—Again!
A Quilter's Ark
Show Me How to Paper Piece

Hand and Machine Quilting/Stitching

Loving Stitches
Machine Needlelace and Other
    Embellishment Techniques
Machine Quilting Made Easy
Machine Quilting with Decorative Threads
Quilting Design Sourcebook
Quilting Makes the Quilt
Thread Magic
Threadplay with Libby Lehman

Home Decorating

Decorate with Quilts & Collections
The Home Decorator's Stamping Book
Living with Little Quilts
Make Room for Quilts
Soft Furnishings for Your Home
Welcome Home: Debbie Mumm

Miniature/Small Quilts

Beyond Charm Quilts
Celebrate! with Little Quilts
Easy Paper-Pieced Miniatures
Fun with Miniature Log Cabin Blocks
Little Quilts All Through the House
Lively Little Logs
Living with Little Quilts
Miniature Baltimore Album Quilts
No Big Deal
A Silk-Ribbon Album
Small Talk

Needle Arts/Ribbonry

Christmas Ribbonry
Crazy Rags
Hand-Stitched Samplers from I Done My Best
Miniature Baltimore Album Quilts
A Passion for Ribbonry
A Silk-Ribbon Album
Victorian Elegance

Quiltmaking Basics

Basic Quiltmaking Techniques for Hand Appliqué
Basic Quiltmaking Techniques for Strip Piecing
The Joy of Quilting
A Perfect Match
Press for Success
The Ultimate Book of Quilt Labels
Your First Quilt Book (or it should be!)

Rotary Cutting/Speed Piecing

Around the Block with Judy Hopkins
All-Star Sampler
Bargello Quilts
Block by Block
Down the Rotary Road with Judy Hopkins
Easy Star Sampler
Magic Base Blocks for Unlimited Quilt Designs
A New Slant on Bargello Quilts
Quilting Up a Storm
Rotary Riot
Rotary Roundup
ScrapMania
Simply Scrappy Quilts
Square Dance
Start with Squares
Stripples
Stripples Strikes Again!
Strips that Sizzle
Two-Color Quilts

Seasonal Quilts

Appliquilt® for Christmas
Christmas Ribbonry
Easy Seasonal Wall Quilts
Folded Fabric Fun
Quilted for Christmas
Quilted for Christmas, Book II
Quilted for Christmas, Book III
Quilted for Christmas, Book IV
Welcome to the North Pole

Surface Design/Fabric Manipulation

15 Beads: A Guide to Creating One-of-a-Kind Beads
The Art of Handmade Paper and Collage
Complex Cloth: A Comprehensive Guide
    to Surface Design
Dyes & Paints: A Hands-On Guide to Coloring Fabric
Hand-Dyed Fabric Made Easy

Theme Quilts

The Cat's Meow
Celebrating the Quilt
Class-Act Quilts
The Heirloom Quilt
Honoring the Seasons
Kids Can Quilt
Life in the Country with Country Threads
Lora & Company
Making Memories
More Quilts for Baby
Once Upon a Quilt
Patchwork Pantry
Quick-Sew Celebrations
Quilted Landscapes
Quilted Legends of the West
Quilts: An American Legacy
Quilts for Baby
Quilts from Nature
Through the Window and Beyond
Tropical Punch

Watercolor Quilts

Awash with Colour
Colourwash Quilts
More Strip-Pieced Watercolor Magic
Strip-Pieced Watercolor Magic
Watercolor Impressions
Watercolor Quilts

Wearables

Crazy Rags
Dress Daze
Dressed by the Best
Easy Reversible Vests
Jacket Jazz
More Jazz from Judy Murrah
Quick-Sew Fleece
Sew a Work of Art Inside and Out
Variations in Chenille

Many of these books are available through your local quilt, fabric, craft-supply, or art-supply store. For more information, call, write, fax, or e-mail for our free full-color catalog.

Martingale & Company
PO Box 118
Bothell, WA 98041-0118 USA

1-800-426-3126
International: 1-425-483-3313
24-Hour Fax: 1-425-486-7596
Web site: www.patchwork.com
E-mail: info@patchwork.com